FORECAST

A manual that combi
forecasting with p.
astrological data and interpreting it correctly.

Also in this series

ASTROLOGICAL COUNSELLING
Christina Rose

ASTROLOGY AND HEALTH
Sheila Geddes

HOW TO INTERPRET A BIRTH CHART
Martin Freeman

MUNDANE ASTROLOGY
Michael Baigent, Nicholas Campion and Charles Harvey

NATAL CHARTING
John Filbey

SYNASTRY
Penny Thornton

FORECASTING
BY
ASTROLOGY

A Comprehensive Manual of Interpretation and Technique

by

Martin Freeman
D.F.Astrol.S.

THE AQUARIAN PRESS
Wellingborough, Northamptonshire

First published 1982
Second Impression 1983

British Library Cataloguing in Publication Data

Freeman, Martin
  Forecasting by astrology.
  1. Horoscopes.
  I. Title
  133.5'4   BF1728.A2

  ISBN 0-85030-297-8

Printed and bound in Great Britain

To Linda and Tara, who were
patient while I wrote.

CONTENTS

LIST OF ILLUSTRATIONS

Thanks to:

Charles Harvey for advice on harmonics and on the Bibliography.

Chester Kemp for his Virgoan checking of the typescript and also for advice on the Bibliography.

Geoffrey Cornelius, Doreen Tyson and Pauline Hayward for advice on the Bibliography.

Sandra Muldowney for typing with speed and long-suffering cheerfulness.

1.
FATE AND FREE WILL

A legend from the Middle East tells how a rich merchant's servant in Baghdad came to his master one day in great consternation. 'Master,' he cried, 'someone bumped into me in the crowded market place this morning. When I turned around I saw it was Death. I caught his eye and he gave me such a strange and terrifying look that I am now in fear of my life. Master, please lend me your horse so that I may flee—with your help I can be far away in Samarra by nightfall.' The merchant was a generous man and, lending the servant a fine horse, he sent him forthwith on his way. Later, the merchant himself went to the market place and saw Death standing in the crowd. 'Why did you frighten my servant this morning and give him such a threatening stare?' 'I did not threaten him,' said Death. 'It was a look of surprise—I was astounded to see a man this morning in Baghdad when I have an appointment with him tonight in Samarra.'

Was the merchant's servant fated to die that night, or could he have exercised his free will and remained in Baghdad? Perhaps Death would have changed his travelling arrangements and kept the appointment anyway. What would have happened if the servant had confronted Death instead of running away? Perhaps he could have negotiated a delay in the timing of the appointment and enjoyed a longer life in return for a gift or a favour, some sacrifice to satisfy the sombre reaper.

The story is a useful introduction to this book, for the central question raised in any discussion about forecasting the future by astrology is to ask how much in life is fated and to what extent human beings have free will. Throughout history, people have speculated and wondered with both fear and curiosity what the future may hold for them. Some choose religious faiths to satisfy and comfort them; others hold totally scientific and rational views;

some seek advice from oracles, planets, prophets, tarot cards or sheep's entrails; yet others question and inquire, searching in the world and within themselves for meaning. Thus, philosophers of every age have dug deep into theories and ideas, and the words describing them, in order to try to find the treasure of understanding.

Billions of years ago, at the creation of the universe, a dynamic pattern was set in motion that to many minds seems entirely predictable. In one small part of the universe, our own little solar system, the moving equilibrium of the Sun, Moon and the planets, swings through space, turning and revolving, a giant machine of cosmic precision. Our computer calculations can tell us, for example, Saturn's position in Libra in 1893 with the same certainty as its future position in Taurus in 1999. From this, one might have some sympathy for the totally fatalistic theories of scientific determinism, for it seems that everything is completely predetermined by efficient and rational causes, eliminating all trace of design. In this context a philosopher would not even allow the use of the word 'predestined', becaue there is no guiding intelligence at work. But reliance on the chance throw of some biochemic cosmic dice to produce such an ordered universe, supporting the complexities of life on at least one planet, involves incomprehensively high odds against its ever happening. They are far greater than the odds against a cat walking on a piano or a monkey playing with a typewriter ever producing a sonata or a sonnet.

Thus grew the intellectual concept of an ordering energy in the universe, something omnipotent but incomprehensible, benevolent and yet destructive—complex enough to receive man's projections and to become a deity. Primitive man saw gods in the Sun, which gave him life, light and warmth, and in the nature mysteries, which gave him food to eat. If the crops grew in abundance, the gods were pleased; if flood or famine struck the land, the gods were angry. As man's intellect grew he refined these theological beliefs, but found that each answer produced ever more questions. St Augustine advised Christians to avoid the concept of 'fate', since it implied that things were determined apart from the will of both God and man; he preferred the words 'providence' or 'predestination'. Aquinas said that providence was the 'ordering of effects' by God. Fate, being subordinate, was the way in which the effects were carried out. Lucretius, however, had earlier condemned fatalism and taught that everything happens according to the laws of Nature, other than which there is no fate. All motion is linked together and each springs from another in a fixed order; but man does have the power of free action to cause a different motion, by the 'swerving of the atoms' in his make-up.

Theologians have always had difficulty in reconciling fate and free will and seem to leave themselves awkwardly somewhere between the extremes of two heresies. If it is heresy to deny God's infinite knowledge and power, then nothing remains outside the scope of divine providence and everything is foreseen by God. But if we deny that man sins freely, then God must be responsible for man's evil—so denying free will is a heresy because it imputes evil to God. Dr Johnson said that he could judge with great probability how a man will act in any circumstance and that his judgement in no way restrains that man. 'God may have this probability increased to certainty,' he added, allowing both fate and free will to co-exist. But Boswell retorted that 'certainty', by definition, removed the man's free will.

Many philosophers have pointed out that a totally fatalistic attitude removes all reason for any moral action in life and almost removes the purpose of living, substituting only a resigned apathy; there can be no distinction between virtue and vice. But none of these brilliant minds has found it easy to prove the existence of free will—'All theory is against the freedom of the will,' said Dr Johnson, 'all experience for it.' The experience and enjoyment of their liberty was alone enough to convince some philosophers of their free will, while others pointed out the difference between involuntary and voluntary actions—the latter being what a man has freely decided to do. 'You say: I am not free,' wrote Tolstoy. 'But I have lifted my hand and let it fall. Everyone understands that this illogical reply is an irrefutable demonstration of freedom. That reply is the expression of a consciousness that is not subject to reason.' But such responses may be merely pure illusion—we want to believe we are free and yet everything we do is fated; even Tolstoy's arm was perhaps pulled up secretly by some scorning Olympian puppeteer. Kant, however, believed that he proved the existence of free will by equating it with pure reason and arguing that consciousness of the moral law infers freedom—but he did think he might be suspected of circular reasoning.

As so often happens, philosophical argument does little more than emphasize or even increase the complexity of a subject, so let us turn back to the Greeks and the symbology in their myths in order to approach the subject from another angle. It is from such ancient stories, told and recorded by those early brilliant minds, that we derive phrases like: 'It's in the lap of the gods', or 'It is bound to happen'—even in modern everyday speech a fatalistic attitude creeps in. Certainly, to the Greeks, the gods held the strings and classical scholars observe the descriptions of binding and knots, of two armies 'tied together' in conflict, in the tension of equal combat. The metaphor is one of a piece of rope drawn tightly by the gods, knotted and encircling the warriors, able to be pulled this way or that with no escape. The bonds were also bounds or limits—very tight and narrow in the example above. Usually such bonding was seen as misfortune and it was only the gods who could untie the bonds. This was particularly true of Zeus, but generally there was an implied moral sanction: usually, what he had bound, under the Olympian rules, he could not unbind. But the gods could be approached appropriately—moving East, in the ancient Hindu *Rig Veda*, there are many prayers to this effect, for example: 'Unloose, unbind the error committed which is attached to my body.'

There are, however, other bindings that bestow blessings, and sometimes a god or goddess would lay the 'girdle of victory' on a warrior or an army. In the Old Testament the psalmist echoes this benevolence: 'It is God that girdeth me with strength and maketh my way straight.' The values of positive binding were taken further in the 'weaving' of spells and in the making of amulets, which were originally cords fastened around the neck or arm and later developed into intricate and complex knots, before eventually including lucky stones and other charms. So within the concept of binding, fatalistic and limiting, we see glimmers of the freedom to counteract misfortune.

More interesting is the metaphor of spinning, which is encountered in many different ancient cultures. The Greeks had the image of the gods sitting with a basket filled with wool at their left hand side, drawing it across their knees or laps and spinning the threads of mortal man's lives, across and down to their right. These threads were either long or short, strong or weak and represented predestined fate. In Nordic mythology, by the side of the great ash tree Yggdrasil that supported the universe, sat the three Norns, giant goddesses of fate. In addition to watering the roots of the tree, their tasks were to sew the web of fate for each mortal. Two were kindly, but the third was cruel and savage, often tearing and spoiling her sisters' handiwork. Greek mythology also included three Fates, the Moirai: Clotho was the spinner, Lachesis the disposer of lots and Atropos was the unchangeable one who cut the thread of life at death. In more recent Lithuanian mythology there were seven Fates. The first spun the thread, the second set up the warp, the third wove the woof, the fourth told tales to tempt the workers to leave off, while the fifth exhorted them to industry and added length to the life. The sixth cut the threads and the seventh washed the garment, giving it to the most high God. It then became the man's winding sheet.

The metaphor becomes more complex when we look further at the weaving that the gods and Fates carried out and we may use the analogy to suggest increasing consciousness in man as what was originally a life thread develops into a length of woven cloth. Weaving by hand was a tedious business. The long warp threads determined the length of the piece of cloth, while the woof or cross threads gave the substance and the quality. The more woof threads there were the tighter the weave and the stronger the cloth, but threading the woof was difficult, even with some form of shuttle. The weaver had to push the thread through the correct opening or, if a primitive loom was used, the shuttle had to be thrown through that opening at precisely the correct moment—'in the nick of time', nick being a small opening.

Thus, we ask, does this grasping of the critical moment and unhesitatingly taking the required action imply that more conscious man, the man whose cloth of life is of a richer quality, has some involvement in his own weaving process? Death is inevitable at some point for every human being, so the threads which the gods spin must always have an end; but perhaps the cross threads, the quality of life, allow us to have a hand in our personal weaving process. To do this we must be alert, so that we are able to throw the shuttle through at that critical moment; we must be conscious and psychologically aware if we are to have a chance of exercising free will and modifying our fate. In John Masefield's poem, 'The Widow in Bye Street', perhaps the immature young man, Jimmy, had more opportunity to avoid his fate than the merchant's servant who fled to Samarra. When Jimmy first met the woman who was later to provoke him to commit murder there was: 'Death beside him knitting at his shroud.' But when he fell in love with her, the die was cast:

Death stopped knitting at the muffling band.
'The shroud is done,' he muttered, 'toe to
chin.'
He snapped the ends and tucked his needles in.

Jimmy, whether he knew it or not, had made his choice.

Psychologically, we have few options in the critical first years of life. Our parents conceive us and bring us into the world and into their environment—rich or poor, peaceful or strained. We inherit their genes and undergo conditioning at their mercy. It is as though the process weaves a twentieth-century cloth of traumas, guilt and repression, fated on the length and breadth of the loom. As we grow older the contents of the unconscious are unknowingly projected out. What we cannot face in ourselves we see in people we dislike; what we cannot find in ourselves we see in those we love. It is only a short step to repeating what ancient man used to do: if good luck came his way, the gods were rewarding him for being good; if the gods were angry and wanted revenge, then he was punished. People's gods today are not the proud deities of old: they are so often insidiously camouflaged in empty values and in hubris. The omnipotent parents of childhood are all too often superseded in later life by the big company employer, the state and government administration, the church, a guru, a group, or even lover or spouse. They, too, can seem to reward a man when he is good and punish him when he is bad. Projections are thrown out, consciousness avoided and personal responsibilities eschewed. It is this level of awareness that finds it comfortable to believe in fate and seeks solace and reasoning platitudes in predictions of the future. Freedom is valued as an ideal, but it may be frightening in reality.

Thus it seems that, although a proportion of our circumstances are fated, there is opportunity for much free will to be exercised—we have the choice. A belief in reincarnation and karma extends the concept of choice far beyond a single life span on Earth. The soul chooses the life—the parents, the environment, the genes, the sex, the gifts and the limitations—all encapculated in the chosen moment that defines the astrological birth chart. These soul choices are made knowingly, as a result of past actions, and so it is perhaps the soul that spins those fated threads and either weaves the woof or stands back and allows the person to try a hand, like an apprentice at the loom.

If we can project, we can also internalize—though it takes more effort—and it is at this point that we can refer this complex and ambiguous balance between fate and free will to the moving planetary trends in astrology. Life is a vehicle for personal growth and, in the wider but unknowable context, growth for the soul. The ancient Egyptians believed the soul was weighed after death, not competitively, but against the feather of Maat—a standard weight for judgement. Modern esoteric belief is that the soul makes its own determination, by reference to the Akashic records. The opportunities for growth are shown by the moving indicators in the birth chart as the years unfold and the timing of these opportunities is precisely laid out at birth. When the warp threads part, we have the opportunity to weave a cross thread of our choice—colour, quality and strength. If we miss the moment altogether, the cloth will be thinner and of less value. But the freedom of choice is definitely there, however much we may feel that fate is in command and ruling with an unkind hand.

Another story, dubious in its mixed mythology, but helpful in its content nonetheless, tells how the God Krishna was worried about the coming influence of Saturn in his life. He decided to escape the demanding lessons of the old schoolteacher and, turning himself into a hippopotamus, hid in a jungle swamp, dank, smelly and dark. After a period of wallowing in the mud, he dragged himself out, cleaned himself up and changed back into his divine form. He met Saturn a little while later. 'Ha, ha,' said Krishna, 'I escaped you this time! I was hiding in a swamp, disguised as a hippopotamus.' 'I know,' replied Saturn quietly. 'I thought you were having quite unpleasant enough a time and there was no need for me to even come near you.' Krishna had made his choice, but the Saturn effect was realized nonetheless.

When the transits and progressions come, we choose in our lives what we need at the time. We may not be choosing consciously, but we attract the appropriate events and circumstances and react accordingly. If the ego is strong and well developed, and if we are searching consciously for growth, then we may choose a path with our eyes open and walk that path with the enjoyment and reward of positive adventure. Sometimes pain is a necessary experience, the result of a build up of missed or avoided opportunities for confrontation earlier in life (and perhaps some may even have come from a previous life); but when the *meaning* of the experience is consciously understood and assimilated, then much progress has been made.

In *The Secret of the Golden Flower*, C. G. Jung wrote, on the subject of those patients who genuinely achieved positive growth:

> The new thing came to them from obscure possibilities either outside or inside themselves: they accepted it and grew with its help . . . If it came from outside, it became a profound inner experience; if it came from inside, it became an outer happening. In no case was it conjured into existence intentionally or by conscious willing, but rather seemed to be borne along on the stream of time.

The moving planetary indicators in the unfolding birth chart are like those 'obscure possibilities'. We cannot will them or control them because they are predetermined, but the way we react to them and accept their correspondences into our inner and outer lives is entirely free. This is the narrow path which lies between fate and free will and which is the route to fulfilment, growth and happiness.

2.
CYCLES

Astrology is intimately associated with time. The birth chart is an encapsulation of a moment in time, animation suspended and yet bursting with unlimited potential, like a ripe seed pod or a new bud in spring. The unfolding and realizing of that potential is the movement of time within the birth chart as life develops, like the first movement of the hands and pendulum of a fully wound clock or a frozen image on a video screen springing into life. In this context time should not be seen as linear: it is better thought of as cyclic—either it relentlessly repeats a similar pattern or, as a spiral of cycles within cycles, with each vortex pattern contributing to an even greater cycle, it can be an overall scheme of growth and development.

Many people believe that an individual life is just one part of a much greater pattern of experience, but most personal astrology is concerned only with that single life. Thus, astrological forecasting for an individual is an examination of the cycles moving within that life as seen in the chart. Symbolically, the cycle of the seasons corresponds with life. It starts with a time of growing from small beginnings and leads to ripening and harvest; an autumn of beauty follows, with its subtle colourings—nourishment comes from earlier productivity and seeds that were planted for the future. Finally, with winter, there is quiet preparation for slumber. Another familiar cycle is the period of day and night. There is the progression from embryonic gestation before dawn, sunrise-birth, then the midday peak of achievement preceding a productive or enjoyable afternoon. There is an element of withdrawal or sacrifice after that peak, which allows the quiet relaxation of evening before the darkness of night-death, an unknown adventure we must all take. C. G. Jung said that death is psychologically as important as birth and, like it, an integral part of life.

That beautifully poetic expression 'the secret hour of life's midday' also comes from C. G. Jung and in this context it reminds us that we do not always know at which point we are on any particular cycle in our lives. Similarly, although there will always be a spring, a summer, an autumn and a winter each calendar year, nature has its own timing. Summers may be long and dry or, often in Britain it seems, frustratingly short. Spring sometimes blossoms early with a naive innocence, only to be crushed by a late frost. There is a Greek word *kairos*, which leads us to the concept of qualitative time. Years of linear calendar time may pass; cycles may repeat with the unchanging precision and predictability of a quartz clock's hour hand, and yet no real progress or growth is achieved. Then in a certain hour, week, month, or whatever time span—a period of significant or rare quality—it is as though years of calendar time have elapsed and disproportionate experience has been gained. *Kairos* is a critical point or a moment of truth and relates to the similar concept discussed in the previous chapter.

We can also consider the tides of the ocean. They ebb and flow daily and, as spring and neap tides, wax and wane with the rhythm of the Sun and Moon's gravitational pull. Within this pattern, the waves rise and fall with infinite variety; but it is impossible to chart the progress of any individual droplet of water—one of them may remain contained in a perpetual dance in a small lagoon, another may travel vast distances on its journey, amassing a wealth of liquid experience through watery adventures. The cycles in the birth chart and their possible developments in life are similar.

Returning more specifically to our subject, there are a considerable number of widely diverse cycles in astrology and there are the means to calculate their rhythms with great accuracy. Each astrologer can have access to the information and can know the exact timing of their movements, but the quality and degree of their correlations in human life are never so certain. For example, scientists have calculated the span of sunspot activity as being 11.11 Earth years, but their nature and effects are obscure. Saros cycles, once used by the Babylonians and Chaldeans as a correlation of sixty days with sixty years, are more usually the description given to a complex period of eclipse sequences. There are nineteen different cycles each of 18 years 11 days (approximately), which overlap and intertwine with each other. The Chaldeans and other early astrologer-astronomers used these cycles extensively in their predictions and forecasts for nations and their rulers, but modern astrologers do not generally use them and little research has therefore been done on their correlations in the twentieth century. Professional astrologers today tend to concentrate on personal consultations and have little time available for working on cycles of this breadth and magnitude. Perhaps this will change when government leaders once again start taking an interest in the influences of the Sun, Moon and planets on national and international activities (see bibliography and the section on Lunations in Chapter 4).

The Sevenfold Quality of Cycles

The number seven and its symbolism can be regarded, very loosely, as the basis of cycles in astrology. To a numerologist, every number has important meaning, but the number seven has wider and more complex associations than any other number. These stretch from the mundane seven days in a week to the philosophical seven ages of man and the esoteric seven rays. Seven is made up of the sum of trinity and quaternity $(3 + 4 = 7)$, the Qualities (cardinal, fixed and mutable) and the Elements (fire, earth, air and water). Before the invention of the telescope the solar system was seen as comprising seven bodies—Sun, Moon and the planets out to Saturn. (These have been given astrological correspondences to most of the other sevenfold divisions.) There are seven notes in the diatonic scale, colours of the spectrum, wonders of the world, deadly sins and virtues. There are seven Japanese Gods of Luck, Shichi Fukujin, and in mythological legend the 'Seven against Thebes' attacked the seventh gate of the city, which was defended by seven Theban heroes. It almost sounds like the title of an epic adventure movie and reminds us of *The Seven Samurai* and *The Magnificent Seven*—even Ingmar Bergman's haunting *The Seventh Seal*. In all cultures there is something special about a seventh son—usually he is said to possess remarkable healing powers. The list is long, and no doubt the reader will think of other examples.

How does this loose sevenfold quality apply? Saturn takes 29½ years (average) to make one complete circuit of the zodiac. This equates with a period of just over seven years to transit each quadrant of three signs. Thus, around every seven years Saturn will make a major aspect to its natal position—square, opposition or conjunction. Uranus takes 84 years to travel around the zodiac, averaging seven years in each sign. 'The days of our age are three score years and ten', sang the psalmist, but with increased life expectancy today there is a more satisfactory completeness about a lifespan of seven times twelve years. It must be emphasized that this in no way suggests that people who survive the biblical seventy years are likely to drop dead at the time of their Uranus return. It is a symbolic statement, which shows that when a life has been lived in relative harmony with the cycles, after the 84-year Uranus cycle there is an opportunity to enjoy the fruits of a well-rounded term of living. C. G. Jung is a good example of this. Although he was controversial to the medical establishment, his theories of analytical psychology were published formally in his collected works for all to read. When these were completed, he agreed right at the end of his life to write an autobiographical book *Memories, Dreams and Reflections*. It is different in style and flavour—the last words of an old man who had achieved much in his 84 years. He died aged 86.

Neptune and Pluto returns never happen in a human life time—their cycles are 165 years and 248 years respectively. Thus, Neptune averages two seven-year periods in each sign. Pluto averages 21 years, but because its orbit is so eccentric it can remain in one sign for as long as 33 years or as short as 13 years (e.g. 1851-1884 in Taurus, 1983-1995 in Scorpio). The periods are approximate because retrograde motion can produce two or three entries and exits to and from signs. These slow movements of the outer planets have more relevance in mundane astrology—the astrology of the collective—and will be covered in some detail in a forthcoming book in this series. But to give examples, the development of popular music and the film industry, both ruled by Neptune, can be observed to follow fourteen-year cycles as that planet moves from sign to sign. The 'talkies' and a preoccupation with technique almost obsessed the film industry when Neptune was in Virgo (1928-1943). Heavy rock music, with its emphasis on sex, drugs and darkness, correlated with the transit of Neptune through Scorpio, the sign of extremes (1957-1971). When the planet moved into philosophical Sagittarius, George Harrison's *My Sweet Lord* topped international charts for a record number of weeks. In 1968 Uranus moved into Libra, the sign associated with relationship, and later in 1971 Pluto followed. These two meta-morphosis creating planets have never both been in Libra at the same time this millennium and it has been a period of change in society's attitudes to close personal relationships. Divorce is no longer the disgrace it used to be, extra-marital cohabitation is widely accepted and homosexuals are increasingly able to live openly together. These correlations are very broad and must be seen in a wide perspective, for there are numerous modifying factors. A significant one has been the mutual aspects made between these three outer planets during the early 1970s and the 1980s, but this takes us into more detail than is relevant here.

The 12-year Jupiter cycle is less important and does not fit into the broad sevenfold pattern under discussion—although within the 84-year Uranus cycle there are seven returns of Jupiter. There are, however, three more cycles which do correlate with the pattern. First, we can examine the early years of life. The intense and rigid tuitional style of the Jesuits before their changes and reforms in the 1960s led to their being attributed with the dictum: 'Give me a child until he is seven and he is mine for life'. Any psychologist would agree that these early years, especially the first two or three, are critical in terms of conditioning and early development. Astrologically, we can correlate this to the intensification or weakening of natal aspects by progression and direction (see Chapter 3). Remember that natal aspects are always relevant throughout life and their development by progression is only an overlay of influence, a modification to something already in existence. Nevertheless, a natal conjunction between the Sun at 10° of a sign and Saturn at 16° will, by progression, move to exactness during the first six years of life. If the positions are reversed, the progressed aspect will weaken and move out of orb in the first two years, but by direction Saturn will move onto the Sun in six years. An orb commonly used for major aspects is ±8° and technically a wide conjunction at birth would take eight years to move to exactness, so the sevenfold theme does not apply precisely. Nor is it intended to, for the quality of seven in cycles is a broad concept loosely supported by astrological realities, not one to be reduced to computerized predictability. Perhaps we should reconsider 7° orbs!

Our second addition is another slightly obscure cycle that also fits into the pattern—the 30° movement of the progressed Sun. In approximately thirty years the progressed Sun will make an aspect of some sort to every other planet—indeed to every point on the chart. Some planets may receive two aspecting contacts if semi-squares and sesqui-quadrates are considered, others may only receive a gentle semi-sextile. For example, the Sun at 2° Aries makes no natal aspect to Jupiter at 10° Gemini (Figure 1). Around age eight, the progressed Sun sextiles Jupiter, but at around age

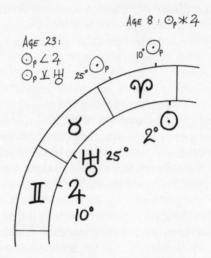

Figure 1.   Progressed Sun Cycle (Example 1).

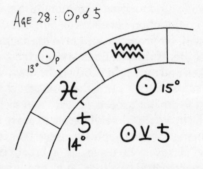

Figure 2.   Progressed Sun Cycle (Example 2).

twenty-three it will make a semi-square. If Uranus is at 25°
Taurus, the progressed Sun will be in semi-sextile to it in the same
year. This thirty-year cycle causes the planetary contacts to repeat
throughout life, but the quality of the contacts will change with
differing aspects. The sevenfold correspondence is not exact, but it
comes closer if we also consider 1° or even 2° orbs—natal Sun at
15° Aquarius semi-sextile Saturn at 14° Pisces will be within orbs
of conjunction in 28 years at 13° Pisces by progression (Figure 2).
  Lastly, the Moon takes 27.32 days to travel around the zodiac

and therefore the progressed Moon cycle is just under 28 years. So there are three cycles that emphasize this 4×7 period of time—progressed Moon, progressed Sun by sign and transiting Saturn.

The Saturn Return

Of the various 28-30-year cycle indicators, Saturn is the most definitive. It is the strongest and the easiest to observe. Any attempt at a complete understanding of the Saturn return must be preceded by study of Saturn in the birth chart. This planet represents lessons to be learned in life and these are shown by sign and house placings, by rulership and by the aspects made to other planets and the angles. The first Saturn return is the first major examination set by the old schoolteacher. Every possible mood of Saturn has been presented and experienced in each transiting aspect during its first cycle—those are the preparatory lessons leading up to the examination. The Saturn return is the astrological coming of age; age eighteen and twenty-one have little relevance in this context.

Thus, in the individual's life at this time, there is likely to be a testing relating to whatever Saturn refers natally. It may concern all such emphasized areas of life, or it may focus on only one or two. The tests may come through other people or in external events; in dark moods or in inner striving. It depends on either the individual's ability to contain the tension within and allow growth and transformation to take place, or his need to externalize the experience, projecting difficulties onto other people so that they are the apparent cause of the problems and personal responsibility is supposedly excused. But Saturn is Lord of Time; he is patient and will wait until the next return around age fifty-six to fifty-nine—or there are the seven-year sub-cycles within the period, the squares and opposition to the natal position, when he may set intermediate examinations. Of these, the first square after the return is normally the most important because it presents the opportunity to tie up any loose ends that may have been left undone at the return itself.

As with all transits, there will be one or three points in time when it is exact, depending on retrograde motion. But with any slow moving planet, particularly where these important life cycles are concerned, it is the period within orbs that is much more relevant than the days of exactness. For example, Saturn in the birth chart at 25° Libra had a relatively short return in 1982, extending little

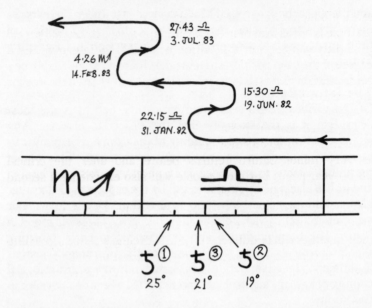

Figure 3.   Transiting Saturn: Movement and Stations in 1982 and 1983.

later or earlier than the month of October. Saturn at 19° Libra was
affected during November-December 1981, March-April and
August-September 1982: here the effects undulated over nearly a
year. But if natal Saturn is at 21° Libra there would have been an
especially concentrated period because a station was made at the
end of January 1982 on 22.15° Libra. The period was intense from
December 1981 to April 1982 and lingered on until August,
September 1982. (See Figure 3. For full clarity, please consult the
ephemeris.)

Clearly, the 25° Libra example is the most lenient Saturn return.
This can be an opportunity to escape, to heave a sigh of relief and
continue on Ophelia's 'primrose path of dalliance', but it is more
advisable to grasp the moment and work with the Saturn lessons, if
only fleetingly, so that future Saturn transits will be more productive and less demanding. The 19° Libra example has its testing
moments, but it is more likely to represent a whole year of serious
re-evaluation and growth. The first cycle of youth has finished, the
initiation ceremony must be experienced, and then a new level is
reached for the next 28-30-year period. The Saturn return can be
exacting and sometimes unpleasant, but it is potentially one of the

most productive times in a person's life. The third, 21° Libra example is not as fearsome as may be supposed. The overall period is slightly shorter, but the station of transiting Saturn within a degree of the natal position suggests that there must inevitably be a confrontation of what Saturn means in the birth chart. If the lessons are learned the rewards are great, but shirking will be dealt with severely.

The seven-year sub-periods within the Saturn cycle, the squares and opposition, have already been mentioned and can be thought of as very minor Saturn returns before and after the critical 28-30-year point; but most people will also experience a second Saturn return at around age 59 ($8 \times 7 = 56$) and some will also reach the third one at around age 88½ ($12 \times 7 = 84$). The principles of these later returns are exactly the same as the first, but their qualities will be different. The first cycle is a period stretching from innocence, through learning and preparation, to an initiation into adulthood, which occurs at the first return. The second return is the point at which a mature person moves into the last phase of life and prepares, in an optimistic Jungian sense, for death. Life has been lived for fifty-six years and many things have been experienced. A certain degree of maturity has been achieved, either by being bruised and battered for a prolonged term in the lower classes of the school or by working diligently in the psychological environment of life so that a university standard has been reached. In either case there is still opportunity for development at the second Saturn return.

The remaining years of life can be a fulfilment of creative achievement, happy retirement, mature marriage partnership, enjoyment of grandchildren, an Indian summer and a golden autumn. Other people unfortunately allow winter to come early—a woman who cannot accept the menopause, a man who will never achieve his impossible career ambitions, manipulative dependency on a son or daughter, loneliness, tranquillizers, anti-depressants, physical illness and an increasing fear of death. For an extreme case in the second example, the confrontation required for any change to take place at the second return may be too much to contemplate, but more generally life's experiences will have forced a certain level of maturity and it is usually possible to achieve some degree of breakthrough at this return. The third Saturn return correlates with the completeness of a life mentioned in the context of Uranus' 84-year cycle, but obviously does not prevent years of happy living thereafter.

The Progressed Moon Cycle

Movement of the progressed Moon is normally very slightly faster than transiting Saturn and the effects of its cycle are much gentler. The Moon's principles are receptivity, fluctuation and response. Its cycle correlates with potential sensitivity to external events and to other people, and it therefore has to do with an individual's reactions to the environment. Progressed Moon conjunct natal Moon occurs a little before the Saturn return and gently prepares the ground for any seeds that will fall. In certain circumstances, when the Moon's and Saturn's speeds are similar, Saturn 'chases' the Moon and a natal conjunction, square or opposition can be prolonged and strengthened by progression over a number of years.

Other important cyclic periods are indicated as the progressed Moon reaches the angles, the Sun and the progressed Sun—the last being a 'progressed' New Moon. Saturn transits can also be considered in this way and both are mentioned again in the chapters on progressions (see Chapter 3 under Moon) and transits (see Chapter 4 under Saturn).

The Uranus Cycle

Although we all hope to reach and enjoy the Uranus return at age 84, the more relevant consideration in this cycle is the opposition of Uranus to its natal position, the half-cycle. It occurs on average at age 42 (6×7) and represents what is often called 'the mid-life crisis'. Remembering that in Chinese the character for 'crisis' is identical to that for 'opportunity', the Uranus half-cycle is the opportunity for a mid-life re-evaluation. All planets have some degree of irregularity in their orbits and this is why cycles may vary from their astronomical averages and why the sevenfold correlation is not numerically perfect, though nevertheless symbolically valid. Uranus is no exception. The table below shows that the half-cycle varies from age 38 to age 45 and it is interesting from a world sociological point of view to note that it is people born in the late 1930s and in the 1940s and 1950s who are stimulated to re-evaluate their lives earlier than their predecessors. These people, growth accelerated in a Uranian greenhouse, will potentially be operating at peak output in planet Earth's critical period 1980-2000.

Year of Birth	Age Span of Uranus Half-Cycle
1900	43-45
1910	43-45
1920	41-43
1930	39-42
1940	38-41
1950	38-40
1960	39-42

The period, normally about a year, when the Uranus opposition is operative, will always provide opportunity for change. For some it is the breaking down of outdated structures in their lives, swaling, burning the old growth so that the new green shoots can receive light unobstructed. This can be uncomfortable, for many of those structures were firmly cemented by parents, teachers and beliefs about society's expectations; but such structures may also be enclosures that hold back the inner urge for progress. For other people these structures can be too strong and, with an obstinate tenacity, they try to climb out of the debris and rebuild exactly the same edifices. More conscious individuals, however, will be able to ride the crest of the wave of change and use the energy of Uranus to transform and diversify where this is appropriate and yet hold on to that from the past which still has value.

The changes indicated by the half-cycle will affect the whole life, but they are likely to focus in those areas affected by Uranus in the birth chart—house, sign, aspects and rulership. There may also be an influence from Saturn opposition Saturn age 42-45 (6 × 7) at the same time. Particular attention should be paid to the house polarity concerned. Lesser influences from Uranus will occur on average every seven years as the transiting planet makes aspects to its natal position. The squares do not have the same importance as the opposition, but it should be noted that the first square of Uranus occurs at around age 21 (3 × 7), an age around when schooling finishes and career begins.

Neptune and Pluto Cycles

Because these cycles are so slow in their movement and because of the eccentricity of Pluto's orbit (Neptune's orbit is almost circular), the cyclic effects of these planets are less important. Pluto transits *on average* to sextile its natal position in 42 years (c.f. half-cycle of Uranus), square at 63 years (c.f. the second square of

Uranus) and trine at the important 84 years—but remember that the actual time scales vary enormously.

Neptune sextiles its natal position at around age 28 and at the Saturn return; the square corresponds with age 42 and the Uranus half-cycle; the opposition occurs around age 84. The following table summarizes these correspondences:

The Sevenfold Correspondences of Aspects from Transiting Planets to their Natal Positions

AGE	♄	♅	♆	♇
7	□	⅄		
14	☍	✶	⅄	
21	□	□	⅄	
28	☌	△	✶	
35	□	⊼		
42	☍	☍	□	✶
49	□	⊼		
56	☌	△	△	
63	□	□		□
70	☍	✶	⊼	
77	□	⅄		
84	☌	☌	☍	△

Figure 4. The Sevenfold Mutual Aspects.

N.B. These are rarely the actual ages when the aspects occur, but they represent the sevenfold quality of the cycles.

When the cyclic aspects of Neptune and Pluto to their natal positions occur, the effect is to create a background of increased Neptune and Pluto influence. In general terms, the former will inspire, refine, spiritualize or confuse and the latter will stimulate inner change, transformation and elimination, but each will act more specifically in terms of natal placing by sign, house, aspect and rulership. The Neptune half-cycle, opposite its natal position, coincides at 84 years approximately with the complete Uranus cycle of change and the third Saturn teaching cycle. It allows a spiritual re-evaluation at the end of life—or it may correlate with utter confusion. The constructive sextile of Pluto to Pluto, theoretically at forty-two years, may positively emphasize the Uranus half-cycle, but the demanding square theoretically coincides with squares in both the Uranus and Saturn cycles at age sixty-three, signalling the challenge of retirement and the autumn and winter of life.

Jupiter Cycles

There are seven Jupiter cycles in the 84-year period, but otherwise this planet does not correlate with the sevenfold pattern. Perhaps it is for this reason that Jupiter cycles do not have greatly significant effects. One of the planet's qualities is optimism and many astrologers indeed hope for more from Jupiter than is usually forthcoming. The effects of a Jupiter return, if noticeable, will depend much on the placing in the natal chart. One is likely to at least feel happily relaxed and optimistic for the week or two when the return is within orbs, but it may also encourage over-indulgence or over-reaching in some form. The most sensible attitude is to see the cycle as one of opportunity. When the return or aspect occurs look for opportunities in life, and try to hold on to them, for many are the times that we either fail to recognize those moments or let them slip through our fingers.

3.
PROGRESSIONS
AND DIRECTIONS

Although there is a cyclic quality in progressions, it is not so obvious as with the cycles discussed in the previous chapter. Secondary progressions equate a day with a year—one daily cycle equates with one solar cycle round the zodiac. Directions, on the other hand, are unrelated to any reality and can therefore be said to be purely symbolic. Some definitions may clarify this:

Transits　　　The actual movement of the planets in the heavens.

Progressions　The actual movement of the planets after birth, but symbolically related to a time-period or cycle in life.

Directions　　A symbolic measure added to all planets, irrespective of speed and direction at birth, related to a period in life.

In justification of secondary progressions' correlating a day with a year of life astrologers frequently turn to the prophet Ezekiel who said in Chapter 4 of his book in the Bible: 'For I have laid upon thee the years of their iniquity according to the number of the days . . . I have appointed thee each day for a year'. But it seems a little over-zealous to take as astrological reality the word of a prophet, biblical or not. Although this symbolic correlation may be enough for some people to accept the theory of progressions without further question, I find it more satisfactory to consider the symbolism in terms of planet Earth itself. A being on the surface of the planet experiences the light and dark of day and night as the planet spins, but Earth as a complete entity experiences a 'day' and a 'night' of six months each as the planet orbits the sun. It may help in understanding this concept to think of the polar axis of rotation alone, without the planet—a line in space making the orbit—or to pretend that the planet is not actually spinning as it travels around the sun. It leads us to speculate that if a year in the life of a human being corresponds to a day in the life of the planet, then perhaps it is possible to calculate progressions for the entity called Earth. The whole solar system is slowly revolving around the galactic centre, so we can surmise that an Earth year may correspond symbolically with a galactic year.

In the more familiar and manageable realms of a mere human life-span, progressions are an entirely personal forecasting indicator, unlike transits, which are collective. For example, the zodiac degree of planet Uranus at any point in time will be exactly the same for every living being on this planet. A progression, however, is dependent on both the individual's birth date and the personal chart drawn up from that information. Because one day after birth corresponds to one year of life, progressions move slowly in the chart. In the chapter on cycles we have observed the relevance of the progressed Sun's movement through a sign, covering about 30° in the chart and 30 days in the ephemeris—both of which correspond to 30 years of life. Thus, the progressed Sun will be within one degree of a sensitive point in the chart twelve months before exactness and twelve months after; there will be a gradual build-up of effect, a rounded peak and a tapering decline. Some people will be more sensitive than others to the influences, feeling the build-up of the applying aspect early or experiencing the separation more strongly—there is no rule, but certainly fore-knowledge can help an individual to prepare for making good use of any forthcoming progression.

From this it will be seen that the Sun is unlikely to progress through more than three signs in a lifetime. If a quadrant house system is used, where the houses may be either greater or smaller than 30° each, a more extensive or more limited journey is possible through the houses. The progressed Sun's movement symbolizes the Quest, the hero's journey or the broad pathway chosen for the life's adventure. Folk legends, fairy tales and myths are full of such quests and journeys and the goals vary enormously—the Golden Fleece, slaying the dragon, the Holy Grail or the lost swan-maiden wife. These quests also include numerous tests or tasks as the journey unfolds—the labours of Hercules are good examples. Similarly, each human life is tested and taught by its Saturn returns, its Uranus cycles and its continuously varying progressed aspects.

The Sun's journey through the signs shows the changing overlays of character and maturity that will evolve during that individual's life. The Sun sign at birth will always remain as a major way of expressing character and consciousness, but it will subtly modify with time. For example, a person born with Sun in 20° Leo will always exhibit that sign's typical generous, confident self-centredness, but around age ten when the Sun moves into Virgo a more meticulous, hard-working, less ostentatious quality will be added. At forty, the graciousness, balance and artistic nature of Libra will also become available, while at around seventy a Scorpionic depth and intensity may tinge the last phase of life. Similarly, the journey through the houses indicates periods of activity focus. A tenth-house Sun at birth shows that the individual will always be concerned with his or her position in the world, an extroverted involvement in the wider issues of the environment. But, depending on that person's capacity to use the astrological influences as they occur, the basic tenth-house focus will modify to a more idealistic group-conscious attitude as the eleventh-house is reached and then to a period of twelfth-house introversion. At some point the progressed Sun may move over the Ascendant and break through into the first-house, bringing a focus of personal strength and individuality, perhaps the culmination late in life of the natal tenth house's promise. The same concepts can be applied to the other planets, but it is the Sun, without any possibility for retrograde motion, that is the most important indicator of the life's quest.

Progressions and Directions Compared

When an astrologer refers to 'progressions' he is almost always referring to secondary progressions and may also be including directions and transits as well. 'I'll have a look at your progressions' means that the astrologer will apply the forecasting techniques he likes to use and will work out what influences are affecting the chart. Methods such as tertiary, minor and converse progressions and primary directions are all less commonly used, but they are described briefly in Chapter 8.

Secondary progressions, taking a day in the ephemeris to equal one year of life, result in movement of about one degree a year for the Sun. The variation in daily motion is between 57' 12" and 61' 11" and it follows that a slow-moving Sun can travel about 38° in forty years, or nearly 41° if moving at its fastest. The progressed

Moon has been mentioned in the previous chapter on cycles and it moves very much faster than the other planets.

Mercury, Venus and Mars have a much more variable rate of travel because of their occasional retrograde motion and therefore they are able to move a greater distance along the zodiac than the Sun in a lifetime. However, retrograde motion can restrict this. For example, Mercury spends between nineteen and twenty-five days retrograde and this means that most people will experience the progressed planet going retrograde at some point in their life. People born soon after Mercury went direct will not experience retrogradation and the planet might travel through four or five signs in a lifetime. This is covered in more detail later in this chapter. The table below shows the periods of retrograde motion for all the planets:

Retrograde Motion

Planet	Average Number of Days Spent Retrograde	Percentage of Mean Synodic Period Spent Retrograde
Mercury	22 (19-25)*	19½%
Venus	42	7 %
Mars	74 (59-81)*	9½%
Jupiter	120	30 %
Saturn	138	36½%
Uranus	152	41 %
Neptune	158	43 %
Pluto	159	44 %

*Range—the other planets vary by only a few days.

Because of their infrequent retrograde motion, Venus and Mars have relatively uniform speeds of travel. Venus moves a little faster than the Sun when direct. Mars is the slowest of all the personal planets; it will take at least forty years to move 30°, but its progressed motion and the aspects it makes will be significant during the lifespan.

Beyond Mars and the asteroids lie Jupiter, Saturn and the three outer planets. Because of their slow movement through the zodiac and the high proportion of their time spent retrograde, their significance by progression is very limited. For example, even the least slow-moving, Jupiter and Saturn, in a long lifetime can only travel through a maximum of half and quarter of a sign respectively. The only practical consideration may be when the effect of a progressed Sun conjunct Saturn, for example, is somewhat prolonged by being followed by the progressed Sun moving into conjunction with progressed Saturn. The aspects of progressed planets to natal planets take precedence over progressed to progressed, but the latter also have an effect.

Most astrologers will agree that secondary progressions are more powerful than any of the various types of directions, but the latter should also be considered. There are three main types of direction—One Degree, Solar Arc and Radix. The basis of all these systems is that *all* the planets and angles in the chart are moved forward by the same amount. Certainly the result is that the outer planets will be much more active with directions than progressions, but this in itself is not a valid reason for using directions. Statistically, there is a much higher probability of aspects occurring by direction and there is also a random quality involved—unlike progressions, which rely on the actual astronomical movement of the planets. If we recall the symbolism and importance of the progressed Sun's movement through the signs, it will be seen that in the case of directions, all the planets will behave in this way, thus devaluing the true progressed motion of the Sun—and the Sun is after all the central focus of the birth chart, the 'Lord and Giver of Life'.

The One Degree system of directing is the lazy man's method. Everything in the chart is moved forward by one degree for each year of life—there is even no need to refer to the ephemeris. It all seems too good to be true. Perhaps advocates of this system are unwittingly relying on the random chance and high statistical probability, referred to above, when they find satisfactory correlations with events. The Solar Arc method has more sense to it—although the method is still subject to the same qualifying comments mentioned already. Here all the planets and angles are moved forward the same distance travelled by the Sun, i.e. the Solar Arc. The degrees involved will not vary much from the One Degree method, but assuming directions do validly correlate with events a difference of a few degrees does mean a few years' difference in timing aspects of aspects. The Radix method is a complex variation on the same theme. All planets, except the Moon, are moved forward at the mean rate of the Sun's diurnal progress—59' 08", known as the Naibod Arc. Some authorities

state that the Moon is moved, for each year, at a rate of 13°
11′—its mean daily motion, known as the minor arc. Tables are
needed if one is to avoid detailed and complex arithmetic, but the
whole system seems to fall between two stools and the logic of
singling out the Moon for preferential treatment (it is allowed to
move at something close to its actual progressed motion) is
perplexing.

In summary, I believe that directions are worth looking at and,
out of the three, I prefer the Solar Arc. I treat them as unquestionably subsidiary to secondary progressions and use only the 'hard'
aspects—conjunction, square and opposition. But each astrologer
must make up his or her own mind. The arguments for and against
progressions and directions are yet another of the grey areas in
astrology and the more valid testing and research that is done, the
better it will be for the evolution and respectability of astrology.

Calculation of Progressions

Progressions are not difficult to calculate. For example, for the 35th
year of a life, count 35 days on from the birthday in the ephemeris
and note the positions of the planets. I suggest doing this around the
outside of the birth chart, preferably in a different colour: in this
way the progressed aspects are easy to see. If the progressed Sun is
conjunct Jupiter, for example, then there will be a year of
opportunity and expansion. As the orb decreases and the aspect
applies, there may be a year's build-up and as the aspect separates a
year's declining effect, perhaps more if progressed Jupiter is a
degree or two ahead of its natal position and the aspect lingers on in
the form of progressed Sun conjunct progressed Jupiter.

These sorts of broad statements about timing are good enough
for general forecasting but need refinement if more accuracy is
required. It is plainly inadequate where the progressed Moon is
concerned, for the movement averages just over one degree per
month and progressed aspects will change quickly. Thus it is
helpful to know the date in the year that corresponds exactly with
the noon positions in the ephemeris (or the midnight positions).
This dispenses with the chore of recalculating the planets for each
year of life in the progressed chart. The date in question is usually
known as the Noon Date, although it will be the Midnight Date if a
midnight ephemeris is being used. Other names include the
Adjusted Calculation Date, Perpetual Noon Date and, sometimes,
the Limiting Date.

The Noon Date must always be calculated from Greenwich Mean Time, which is the time used in the ephemeris, and any calculation method will always involve the time interval between GMT and noon and GMT birth time. The difficulty often experienced in this context is not so much the actual calculation of the Noon Date, but arriving at the correct correspondence between day in the ephemeris and year in the life—it is easy to be wrong by a day and this results in a twelve-month inaccuracy in all progressed aspects.

Stages of Calculation: The stages required for the calculation of progressions are as follows:

1. Find the Noon Date, which will be the time of year when progressed positions in the ephemeris are exact.
2. Find the progressed date in the ephemeris which corresponds with the year under review.
3. Calculate the progressed angles.
4. Calculate the position for the progressed Moon for each month through the year.
5. Compare with the natal chart to see what aspects are formed. Then interpret.

The Noon Date: Whenever tricky concepts are involved, I always prefer to understand the principles rather than to learn rules by rote like a parrot. It helps if one considers the hours before and after the actual birth and compares them to the progressed equivalent, the first few months of life. *Example*: A baby born at 6.00 a.m. in June will have a Noon Date later in the year, because when the infant was a mere six hours old and the noonday Sun was high in the sky, the progressed equivalent would have elapsed by about three months to September (one day = one year, *or*: 24 hours = 12 months). Another baby born at 6.00 p.m. on the same day would have still been in the womb at noon, a progressed equivalent of three months *before* birth; the Noon Date would be around April.

Thus, a birth time before noon will have a Noon Date later in the year and a birth after noon will have a Noon Date before the birthday. The following table will help:

Progressed Equivalents in Time

Ephemeris	*Life*	
1 day or 24 hours	1 year or 12 months	
12 hours	6 months	
6 hours	3 months	
2 hours	1 month	
1 hour	15 days	
30 minutes	7½ days	
10 minutes	2½ days	*approx.*
5 minutes	1 day	

The first method for calculating the Noon Date is thorough, adequately reliable and longwinded. It is purely arithmetical and ensures that the principles of calculation are understood. The other methods are quicker.

A. *The Arithmetical Method*

Birthday: 29 May

Birth Time: 9.55 p.m. GMT

Thus the interval from Noon GMT is 9 hours 55 minutes.

Birth is p.m. and the Noon Date will be before the birth day

From the table above: 9 hours = 4 months 15 days
                                   55 minutes = 14 days

Therefore the Noon Date is 4 months 29 days before 29 May, which is *31 December*.

B. *The Card Method*

1. *Noon Ephemeris*: The purchase of two special tables is necessary. They are available on a single sheet known as the 'Calculation of Noon Date Card'. The instructions are clearly given, but, to explain briefly, the table allows quick reference to give the day number for any date in the year and the day equivalent for any interval. Adding for a GMT a.m. birth and subtracting for p.m. gives the result.

Birthday: 29 May: day number 149 or 514

Interval: 9 hours 55 minutes, the equivalent of 151 days

p.m. Birth: subtract interval from day number (the card conveniently gives the day number itself and the day number plus 365 days—necessary in this example)

514 — 151 = 363 = *29 December* (Noon Date)

2. *Midnight Ephemeris*: If a midnight ephemeris is being used, proceed in exactly the same way, but use an interval from midnight —which will always be subtracted.

Birthday: 29 May: day number 149 or 514

Interval: 21 hours 55 minutes: 334 days

Midnight Ephemeris: subtract interval from day number:

514 — 334 = 180 = *29 June* (Midnight Date)

C. *The Sidereal Time Method*

How I wish I had known about this easiest and fastest method years ago—so much time and work would have been saved! It uses sidereal time and the calculation can be performed, without making any additional entries, by the side of the Ascendant calculation that has already been carried out to find local sidereal time at Greenwich at birth on the standard Faculty of Astrological Studies (FAS) chart form. The stages are as follows:

1. Look up sidereal time for noon or midnight on the day of birth at Greenwich (already on line 1 of natal Ascendant calculation on FAS chart form).

2. Calculate interval between GMT birth time and noon or midnight (on line 2).

    (a) If birth time is p.m. (or if the midnight ephemeris is being used) *subtract* the interval from the sidereal time.

    (b) If birth time is a.m. (using a noon ephemeris) *add* the interval.

N.B. This is the *opposite* to the sidereal time calculation for finding the ascendant in the natal chart.

3. This calculated sidereal time will approximate to the sidereal time for a date in *any* year in *any* Greenwich ephemeris. If a noon

ephemeris is consulted, the Noon Date is given. If a midnight ephemeris is consulted, the Midnight Date is given. Accuracy is to within one or two days, which is perfectly adequate for all normal forecasting work. (If greater accuracy is required, apply acceleration to the interval *in the opposite direction* and proceed as above.) To anyone who has been using traditional methods up till now this method will indeed seem like waving a magic wand.

	Noon Ephemeris			*Midnight Ephemeris*		
Example:	H	M	S	H	M	S
Sidereal time for birth date 29 May 1982	4 (28)	26	45	16 (40)	24	46
Interval (*subtract*—this is the opposite to Ascendant calculation)	9	55	00 —	21	55	00 —
	18	31	45	18	29	46
Optional: including acceleration (*add*—this is opposite to above)		1	38 +		3	36 +
	18	33	23	18	33	22

The Noon Date is taken from any Noon Greenwich Ephemeris:

Example: 1982   29 December   S.T. 18.30.27
            30 December   S.T. 18.34.24
    1950   29 December   S.T. 18.29.29
            30 December   S.T. 18.33.25
    1891   29 December   S.T. 18.32.40
            30 December   S.T. 18.36.36

The Midnight Date is taken from any Midnight Greenwich Ephemeris:

Example: 1996   29 June   S.T. 18.29.25
            30 June   S.T. 18.33.22
    1950   30 June   S.T. 18.29.58
            1 July   S.T. 18.33.55

The Progressed Date: Having found the Noon or Midnight Date, the next stage is to find the correct day in the ephemeris that corresponds to the year under investigation. Merely counting forward from the birthday or, worse still, adding the present age in years to the birthday, leaves room for error. I recommend returning to the months surrounding birth—if the Noon Date is correctly understood at that point, then there will be no ambiguity later.

In our example, the baby was born at 9.55 p.m. GMT on 29 May 1982. The Noon Date is 28 December, so noon in the ephemeris corresponds to the 28 December before birth—noon 29 May 1982 in the ephemeris corresponds to 28 December 1981 in progressed terms; that is, a foetus four months old. The following graphic illustration may help:

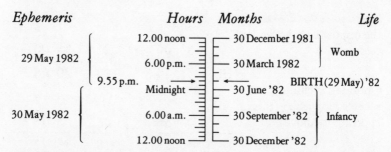

Ephemeris		Hours	Months	Life
		12.00 noon	30 December 1981	Womb
29 May 1982		6.00 p.m.	30 March 1982	
	9.55 p.m.	Midnight	30 June '82	BIRTH (29 May) '82
30 May 1982		6.00 a.m.	30 September '82	Infancy
		12.00 noon	30 December '82	

The Midnight Date is 30 June, so midnight in the ephemeris at the first moment of 29 May 1982 corresponds to 30 June 1981, *before* the birth—indeed before conception.

My own method of ensuring the progressed year is correct is to place the point of my pencil physically in the space between the days printed in the ephemeris, before the birthday for an a.m. birth and after the birthday for a p.m. birth. This enables me to see visually which ephemeris noon refers to which year in progressed terms. Other people will prefer merely to remember 'a.m. birth—later Noon Date: p.m. birth—earlier Noon Date'. Particular care should be taken with births where the GMT date is different from the actual birthday. The golden rule is always to use GMT information —the ephemeris is based on Greenwich, and so should be all your calculations. Once the correct progressed year has been established for this period around the day of birth, it is a simple matter to count the years forward in the ephemeris—for detailed work, including life reviews, it is helpful to note every fifth or tenth year in pencil in the margin.

Calculating the Progressed Angles

Two methods for calculating the progressed Midheaven and Ascendant are shown here. Having found the day in the ephemeris corresponding to the year under investigation, there are two alternatives:

1. *Sidereal Time*: Take the sidereal time for the new date. Carry out an Ascendant calculation in the same way as for the natal chart —add or subtract the interval and the acceleration and then apply the longitude equivalent. Find the Midheaven and Ascendant in a table of houses for the latitude of birth.

2. *Solar Arc*: Calculate the Solar Arc (Progressed Sun minus Natal Sun). Add this to the Midheaven and look up the corresponding Ascendant for the latitude of birth in a table of houses.

Example: (a) Natal Sun   — 8° 10′ Gemini
           (b) Progressed Sun — 27° 53′ Gemini
           Subtract (a) *from* (b) *to give*:
           Solar Arc   — 19° 43′

           Natal Midheaven   — 15°   Sagittarius
           Natal Ascendant   — 23° 29′ Aquarius
           (London table of houses)
           Add Solar Arc to Midheaven to give:
           Progressed Midheaven — 4° 43′ Capricorn
           This Midheaven corresponds to:
           Progressed Ascendant — 12° 19′ Aries

This second method is easier and the small amount of arithmetic needed has to be worked out anyway if Solar Arc directions are also being used. Personally, I feel more comfortable basing the calculation on the Sun's actual movement rather than the less tangible elapse of sidereal time.

R. C. Davison in his book *The Technique of Prediction* states that 'It is possible to predict all the major events of the life by using only directions involving the angles and the Sun.' Although I agree in principle that the angles and the Sun are extremely important indicators, in practical terms for the average amateur or professional astrological consultant, most people do not know their accurate birth times, and therefore the progressed angles are often of limited use only. Remember that a few degrees either way on the angles at birth will result in a few *years* error in timing where progressions are concerned. A rectified chart (see Chapter 8) may purport great accuracy, but even in such a case I treat the progressed angles with caution. As one particularly commercial professional astrologer once said: 'There is a lot of money to be made rectifying other people's rectifications!' However, where the birth time is accurate or where a rectified chart is (as far as possible) proven reliable, the Ascendant and Midheaven are unquestionably of great value in progressions. Many astrologers also progress the house cusps and look for aspect contacts to these points in order to obtain additional forecasting information.

Calculating Progressed Moon Positions: It is quite simple to calculate the monthly positions of the progressed Moon, but the steps are itemized below. Let us assume that we are examining the twenty-first year of the baby born at 9.55 p.m. on 29 May 1982. The Noon Date has been calculated as 29 December and the twenty-first birthday will be 29 May 2003.

1. Progressed date: noon 20 June 1982 corresponds to 29 December 2003.

2. Moon's motion: (a) noon 19 June — 29° 38′ Taurus
(b) noon 20 June — 14° 41′ Gemini
('44° 41′ Taurus')
Subtract (a) *from* (b) — 15° 03′
Thus progressed Moon travels 15° 03′ in the year.

3. Monthly positions: *divide movement by 12* = 1° 15¼′ per month.

29 December,	2002 —	29° 38′ Taurus
29 January,	2003 —	0° 53′ Gemini
28 February,	2003 —	2° 08′ Gemini
29 March,	2003 —	3° 23′ Gemini
29 April,	2003 —	4° 39′ Gemini
29 May,	2003 —	5° 54′ Gemini
29 June,	2003 —	7° 09′ Gemini
29 July,	2003 —	8° 24′ Gemini
29 August,	2003 —	9° 40′ Gemini
29 September,	2003 —	10° 55′ Gemini
29 October,	2003 —	12° 10′ Gemini
29 November,	2003 —	13° 25′ Gemini
29 December,	2003 —	14° 41′ Gemini

Interpretive Comments

The following paragraphs are intended as a basis for working out specific interpretations of the five progressed personal planets in individual charts. Brief delineations of all contacts are given later in Chapter 6, but they must be considered to be of limited use because the circumstances of each individual birth chart cause so many modifications to a standard interpretation. The *principles* of interpreting the progressed movements and the broader considerations already discussed will be of greater use to any student. An understanding of the birth chart as a whole is essential and reference to the meaning *in that chart* of each individual planet must always be carried out.

Progressed Sun: Many of the relevant points have been covered already. Remember the symbolic journey taken by the Sun through certain signs and houses during the life. The basic Sun sign character will be tinged with the later signs, but it is the period of change from one sign to the other which will have the most significance. The houses occupied will show an evolution of life focus, but the actual changeovers will be gradual shifts stretching from the last few degrees of one house to the first few of the next. Remember also the thirty-year cycle of aspects made by the Sun as it progresses through each sign.

The Sun is the urge towards consciousness and self-expression in the chart and its progressed movement represents the dynamic aspect of that urge; opportunities for growth and transformation, confrontations that may be necessary for that person in order to move towards becoming who he or she really is as an individual. Coming to consciousness is not easy and may involve experiencing pain, but the long-term rewards are out of all proportion and the process is far preferable to any short-term apparent comfort, which compares with psychological infancy. Any aspect involving the progressed Sun should be viewed as significant in terms of periods of striving towards the expression of consciousness (or, at any rate, opportunities for it), but the conjunction is the strongest and most important, followed by the oppositions and then the squares.

Progressed Mercury: The mental and intellectual development of the individual are shown by Mercury as it progresses through the chart. Its relevance will be particularly important if Gemini or Virgo, the signs it rules, is rising or, to a lesser extent, if either is the Sun sign. Mercury's expression may subtly change as it moves from sign to sign, most noticeably at the changeover, and its focus will relate to house position, but always the natal house and sign placing will predominate.

Retrograde motion and the stations are frequently of great importance, whether the chart has special emphasis on Gemini and Virgo or not. A majority of people will experience a station of progressed Mercury at some point in their lives and the effect usually lasts for about a year, but may be as long a period as three years. The fact of direct or retrograde motion once the station has passed is generally less notable. There are three sets of conditions involving a station of Mercury:

1. Retrograde at birth, goes direct before age 25.
2. Goes retrograde and direct during the life:
   (a) Retrograde before the Saturn return.
   (b) Retrograde after the Saturn return.
3. Goes retrograde late in life.

If Mercury is retrograde in the birth chart, the intellect and the urge for (or ease of) communication may tend to be introverted, inward-looking or even slightly restricted, depending on its placing in the chart. Whenever progressed Mercury moves direct there will be the opportunity for experiencing an opening-out mentally. In case 1 above, this will normally happen while at school or university and often marks a breakthrough in learning. In case 2, the direct station has a correspondingly positive effect, but in an adult it can have benefits commercially or socially, often coinciding with an expansion of mental interests. Perhaps the most difficult circumstance is where the retrograde station occurs before the Saturn return. The person is still grappling with that first cycle of development towards maturity and Mercury's going retrograde forces mental introversion at a time when natural evolution is towards an emergence from the chrysalis. It often correlates with a difficult period at school. If the retrograde station occurs later in life, as in cases 2(b) and 3, then the experience can be quietly productive and creative, like the fertilization of an ovum in a mental womb. This instance can be unhelpful only where the individual has been living without conscious awareness of his life's natural flow—his psyche's offer to look within is experienced as a threat and mistrust sours the experience.

Progressed Venus and Mars: The movements of Venus and Mars through the horoscope show the development of relationship and initiative respectively, of feminine principle and masculine principle, of passive creativity and active independence. The aspects are more important than the sign and house progressions and the conjunctions are the most significant factors. Because the maximum elongation of Venus is 48° from the Sun, either the Sun will progress onto Venus or, if there is no retrograde motion, Venus will progress onto the Sun at some point in the life. This contact gives a strong probability of an important relationship, often marriage, or it can indicate a blossoming or consolidation of an existing relationship. In some charts the contact occurs at too young an age for it to be used in this way, and therefore a subsequent sextile, for instance, may be a reliable relationship indicator. It is important to remember that Venus has meanings other than relationships in most charts—everyone, including the astrologer, has a romantic and a matchmaker within and it is easy to be blinded by Cupid's spell when interpreting this planet. Mars aspects point to the development or restriction of energy, drive, initiative, courage and sexuality. Neither Venus nor Mars have significant periods retrograde, so it is uncommon to experience a station during life. However, a retrograde Venus at birth is likely to move direct during the life and this suggests that the individual will come out of the shell indicated by that natal Venus. Both Venus and Mars stations should be given due weight in interpretation, if they occur.

Progressed Moon: The Moon creates passive and reactive energies in its relatively speedy progress around the chart. Its effects may not be so strongly obvious as the Sun's aspects or as conjunctions of progressed Mars, for example, but it is always an important indicator. Of course its meaning and temperament in the natal chart must be taken into account; but in general terms, remembering its association with Cancer and with the tides, the Moon's influence will be to do with feelings of security and emotional comfort: we are less affected directly, more carried along like a boat in tidal waters. All aspects made by the progressed Moon are relevant, but the conjunction is the most important, followed by the opposition and then the square.

Progress through the houses draws the individual's vessel into the affairs of each house in turn and requests that the inner, more sensitive relationship with that house is reflected upon. Movement through the quadrants should be noted, particularly the conjunctions with the angles that indicate the start of new cycles—individuality; roots, family and security; partnership; career and extroverted expression in the world—depending on the angle reached. The quality and element of the houses are also relevant:

1. 4. 7. 10:	Angular	= New initiatives
2. 5. 8. 11:	Succedent	= Consolidation
3. 6. 9. 12:	Cadent	= Distribution
1. 5. 9:	Fiery	= Activity, creation and extroversion
2. 6. 10:	Earthy	= Practicality, reality and duty
3. 7. 11:	Airy	= Concepts, ideas and planning
4. 8. 12:	Watery	= Sensitivity, depth of feeling and introversion

Movement through the signs is usually less important, but may present slight changes in emotional expression, particularly around the time of the actual changeover. Progressed Moon conjunct either natal Sun or progressed Sun (the latter is a progressed New Moon) are aspects which each indicate the start of a new cycle of experience, depending on the meaning and placement of the two lights in the birth chart.

4.
TRANSITS

The principles behind transits are much more straightforward than progressions. Here we are considering the planets in their actual position in the zodiac at any given point in time. When a planet moves over an important degree in the birth chart (e.g. Ascendant or Sun) or makes an aspect to that degree, then the energy of the transiting planet will be focused on that particular part of the birth horoscope and will affect it accordingly. Transiting planets move relatively quickly, unlike progressions, and therefore they are often associated with events and specific happenings in life rather than the background influence given by progressions.

However, events and happenings can occur in many different ways or on different levels and the effects of transits are not always immediately obvious. There will always be an 'event' occurring at the time of the transit, but it may quite likely be happening deep within the individual and may not show itself in the outer world until some time, perhaps years, after the actual transit—this later manifested event being triggered off by some other transit or an aspect of the progressed Moon. These levels of inner and outer reality can be looked at in three ways. In the first instance there is no apparent effect. The individual will be operating at a low consciousness, unwilling to confront life's issues and preferring to exist in a psychologically anaesthetized state. Thus the energy of the transiting planet is wasted and the opportunity for growth and development is apparently lost—but the transit did occur and its influence is stored somewhere within the psyche. Later in life, under some other astrological conjunction, a relevant happening will occur, but one which is strengthened or even aggravated by the fact that the energy made available by the first transit was repressed.

The second possibility is much the most common and is the openly straightforward correlation between the transit and an event in the life. Because there are so many different permutations and possibilities associated with the combination of two planets (e.g. houses occupied, houses ruled, relevant natal aspects and, to a lesser extent, the signs involved) there are many different events that can happen, all of which will be valid. Always remember that human beings are not actually at the mercy of external forces—we create the circumstances that we need or deserve or that are relevant to our development. The statement: 'He had an accident' implies that the accident happened to the individual, whereas it is more likely that 'he happened to the accident'—and it is certainly more appropriate to think of the event in this way. Certain transits may validly correlate with accidents, but it is not always necessary for such transits to manifest in this way. The occurrence of illness and unfortunate events often suggests that the individual has not faced up to something in his life and the only way he can be shown reality (perhaps a distasteful reality) is through 'misfortune'. A simple example is the workaholic who disregards all the warning signals of overstrain and then crashes the car or slips a disc.

In this second possibility for the working out of inner and outer realities, we have discussed examples that are not a great deal more conscious than the first instance, in which the transit was apparently without effect. But that short-term supposed comfort—apparently 'getting away with it'—stores up future distress and it is far preferable to start to come to consciousness, even if it means experiencing one of life's little knocks. However, the same transit could correlate just as validly with more positive events. For example, Saturn transiting conjunct the Sun may indeed bring illness, but it may also bring the mother-in-law to stay—and that may be the occasion you negotiate an uneasy truce and actually learn to get on with the old dragon! This transit could also mean pressures of extra work that cannot be avoided, perhaps even in the form of promotion and extra responsibility within one's employment.

The third possibility is again where there appear to be no outside events that correspond to the transit. Here the individual has contained the energy within his own alchemical retort and he concentrates it in his own inner development. The Saturn Sun contact mentioned above would no doubt bring a serious attitude to life and quite possibly a sombre austerity, but it would be a state of mind necessary to allow the individual to focus constructively on the demands of that period in his psychological evolution.

Our reaction to transits reflects our relationship with our environment and with the collective. As shown in the previous chapter, progressions are very personal, but they are broad and prolonged in their effect. Transits have a quality of greater immediacy, but they do relate to the collective—everyone on Earth is experiencing the same movements of all the planets, even though each separate birth chart is affected individually and differently. The three levels of inner and outer reality show how people at their various stages of consciousness and personal development will draw differently on the environment, via the transits, for the experiences they need—instant or delayed, crude or subtle, constructive or unsettling. The simple variable of a person's age must also be taken into consideration. A transit of Jupiter, although short-lived and not strong in its effect, is a good example. Early in life there may be stimulus to travel, whilst the same transit in an older person could encourage mental travel—deeper thought, mature study, an interest in philosophy or religion. Late in life the transit could correlate with a happy final journey and a release from life.

The collective effects of transits should not be ignored. People of different races or nationality will react variously to the psychological and environmental pressures that correspond with a particular transit; socio-economic groupings and levels of education will also be relevant. Marriage and relationships are the most clear examples. In a marriage where the man and the woman are having difficulties, let us assume that Uranus or Pluto is transiting over Venus or is moving into the seventh house. In a fervent Muslim society, infidelity may be punished by death; the devout Roman Catholic would be expected to endure the marriage and seek comfort and salvation through prayer; the nominally Church of England couple might decide to separate and divorce— more quickly and easily if they are financially well off and if they do not become greedy or resentful. The poorly-educated working class couple might experience the transit with violence and escapist drinking, while a middle-class couple with a more fortunate background could use the astrological energies to seek a solution through marital therapy or analysis. If the example had occurred a hundred years ago, the Victorian ethic would have forced a very different reaction than today—even breaking off a betrothal in those days was an unprecedented scandal. Much further back in history, King Henry VIII would have had his wife beheaded or, in the French court of *le grand siècle*, the marriage would have remained unmoved in its social façade, but the upheavals would have occurred amongst the lovers, the liaisons and the intrigues behind the scenes.

The Interpretation of Transits

Remembering that transits are collective and that the birth chart is individual, it can be seen that it is the planet transited on which the spotlight falls and which is given the opportunity for work to be done on whatever that planet represents in the chart. This also applies to angles and houses. The transiting planet in the sky determines the colour of the spotlight or the character of the opportunity for development work. Movement through houses should always be observed, even if there is no transiting aspect occurring, for this will show where the energies of the different planets—collective and environmental energies—will be concentrating for that period in terms of the individual person's experience. Movement through the signs is less relevant, although when a transiting planet enters the Sun sign, rising sign or other strongly emphasized sign, the resonance that this creates may possibly be felt right through the period until it leaves the sign. It is possible for this to happen both in the case of a highly attuned individual, with a developed sensitivity, and where the person is living less as an individual and more under the influence of collective forces.

The Personal Planets: Transits of the Sun, Moon, Mercury, Venus and Mars move too quickly to be of great importance in astrological forecasting. If very detailed work is being carried out, these transits may be considered and can be helpful in determining day-to-day passing influences, but where broader, life-developing investigations are concerned they are rarely relevant. The Sun sign columns in the popular press rely on these transits, treating the twelve signs as solar houses counted from the Sun sign. Certainly every little event, mood, thought, happenstance, shift or episode that occurs in the course of a day will have its astrological correlation—minor aspects, involving minor points on the chart, that apply and separate in the space of a few moments. But such a plethora of minutiae would tax the capabilities of even the most expert computer programmer and I doubt that computerization would be worth the trouble, even assuming it was possible.

A transit of Mars can often be the activity stimulator that

energizes a certain point in the birth chart and prompts other longer-acting indicators into operation and Mars through the houses can sometimes be observed to correlate with increased activity in that sphere of life. The movement of the Sun and Moon over the angles and other sensitive degrees in a chart may occasionally be seen to present a focus of sensitivity, for a short period, but they are ephemeral influences. It is rare for Mercury and Venus to be noticeable by transit. However, if one is looking for the best day to carry out some undertaking, as in electing a chart, the daily transits should certainly be taken into consideration.

There are two instances where these daily movements are more important. First, the stations of any planet should always be noted—it is a good idea to underline them in the ephemeris and some astrologers also mark the whole retrograde period. This is especially important in the case of Mars, which can truly appear to manifest mediaeval malevolence if its station falls on a sensitive degree. Again it must be emphasized that misfortune is by no means inevitable. Awareness of the stationary aspect allows the individual to take care during the few days involved, being sensible rather than paranoid and avoiding such pastimes as rock-climbing and Russian roulette! Such concentrated energy can always be channelled usefully. The stations of Mercury or Venus should be seen as emphasizing the principles of the planet in the context of the birth chart, with any direct station being easier to use constructively than the retrograde station.

The second instance where the fast-moving transits may be important is when there are mutual aspects. The specific case of a full or new Moon is discussed later in this chapter, but when Mars is conjunct the Sun, Moon, Mercury or Venus, for example, and the degree aspects a sensitive point in the birth chart, then more notice can be taken of the transit. The diligent astrologer, paying homage to Virgo, will be aware of the times when the transiting slower-moving planets make aspects to the transiting personal planets, because this will modify the influences. Mars conjunct Saturn transiting the Sun suggests frustration and difficulty, whereas Mercury conjunct Saturn making the same transit implies a few day's opportunity for study and constructive mental work. If Venus transits the Sun while Jupiter transits in square, a day of enjoyable indulgence is a possibility; if it was Mars transiting conjunct the Sun in the same circumstances, then the day would be highly energized, and the individual could achieve a lot, but have difficulty in knowing when to stop.

Jupiter: The very idea of a transit of Jupiter brings out the optimist in all astrologers. Sadly, the jovial Uncle-god frequently promises more than he delivers. Certainly, the duration of the effect is short-lived. A station of Jupiter making an aspect may have an influence for up to a couple of months, but when moving at its fastest the period is reduced to two weeks at maximum. Thus, it is not difficult to miss the effects of a Jupiter transit.

The key to interpretation is that Jupiter expands and opens whatever it touches. It brings a feeling of increment and abundance, not necessarily tangible benefit itself, more the *opportunity* for it. An unlocked door has no relevance to a man unless he opens it and passes through the doorway—opportunities have to be taken when they occur. Indeed, they often need searching out and this fact no doubt led Francis Bacon to say: 'A wise man will make more opportunities than he finds'. Some birth charts suggest that the individual will have more good fortune than other people, that less sweat and tears need flow in the achievement of purpose and ambition; but even in such cases a Jupiter transit will rarely offer the Golden Goose, the philosopher's stone, or the Irish sweepstake win and drop it into the lap. It is much more likely to create a psychological environment of openness and understanding, which can make it possible to find a symbolic equivalent of the fairy tale goose that laid golden eggs. That story is encountered throughout the world and has many variations, but the moral is always the same —that we should count our blessings and not be too greedy.

A Jupiter transit may merely mean that we 'felt good' that week or it may coincide with travel. But it is more relevant to consider it as opportunity for expanding the scope of one's existence at that time, thereby enabling the benefits to extend and live on long after the actual transit is completed. There is opportunity for broadening one's mental concepts and understanding and this can have ramifications like a chain reaction, which may well end in a tangible piece of apparently 'good luck'. Consider the progress of the first creative spark of an idea, which eventually becomes concrete reality. Ideas become ideals and thoughts in an individual's mind; energy follows thought and energy is the raw material of any tangible action or created physical object. Where the birth chart shows a more restricted or cautious character, Jupiter can bring self-assurance and the confidence to move forward. Often attitudes to religion and philosophical subjects are fertilized and later grow to enrich the life.

Expansion can also be inflation, implying exaggeration, and it follows that a Jupiter transit may encourage excess, over-indulgence and over-optimism—too much of a good thing. The waistline may increase with over-enjoyment of rich food, judgement may be impaired or duties may be neglected. The car salesman would rub his hands in delightful anticipation if he knew his customer had, for example, Jupiter transiting opposite natal Sun. The customer would be liable to spend more than he intended on his new car—but he would also be likely to have a lot of fun with the new possession.

Jupiter spends about a year in each sign and therefore may remain for a similar period in each house, but this will vary enormously depending on the size of house transited. Thus there is the potential for enjoyment, opportunity and expansion in the affairs of that house during the time of the transit.

Saturn: The cyclic importance of Saturn and the Saturn return have been discussed in Chapter 2, but similar principles apply in all Saturn transits. In the birth chart, this planet shows lessons to be learned and its qualities have much in common with the stricter type of schoolteacher—duty, hard work, austerity, restriction, stability and maturity. The transits of Saturn are like examinations. No examination is likely to be a gala of merrymaking, but if we have worked hard and do our best when the time comes, the rewards are long-lasting. It is when the lessons are shirked and the exams are poorly handled that the old schoolteacher raps our knuckles with his ruler.

More than any planet, it is vital to understand the meaning of Saturn in the birth chart in order to interpret the transits adequately. The planet's principles of restriction, limitation, duty and discipline will apply by natal sign, house and aspects. We can grit our teeth and work with this energy, sometimes uncomfortable but always highly constructive, or we try to evade it. The latter is not only non-confrontive, but also an unconscious and short-term reaction. There are, broadly, two ways in which this may happen: either we succumb to Saturn's pressures, lacking confidence and feeling insecure, with the weight of the world on our shoulders; or we over-compensate and aggressively try to cover up the feelings of inadequacy. Both these reactions will result at least in a person's operating well below full potential and more often lead to difficulties in life sooner or later. The only way of working with this planet is to confront its influence—and the opportunity for this confrontation is given by its transits. The experience may not always be easy or pleasant and this is why Saturn has its severe reputation.

Once natal Saturn is understood and accepted, and once the decision is made to work as constructively as possible in the learning process, then the transits can be viewed positively and in many cases welcomed. It is quite possible to internalize the image of the old schoolteacher who sets exams and to use the transits to examine oneself and slowly develop the teacher within. This is within the capacity of every human being, but not all people allow that inner teacher to live and grow to full contributive capability.

Saturn enables us to focus and concentrate on whatever it is touching, both natally as well as by transit. Being an essentially earthy planet it brings opportunity for practical and realistic activity, sometimes slowing down our rate of progress so that the job can be done more thoroughly and with more meditative reflection. In an impulsive chart, or one with a weak Saturn (hence a tendency for undisciplined behaviour) or a chart which lacks the earth element, these transits may indeed create feelings of frustration, delay or restriction; but the purpose and value behind them is to provide opportunity to confront the lack of discipline inherent in the character.

Saturn's capacity to provide a constructive focus is also relevant in its movement through the houses. Much of what has already been said in the chapter on cycles applies here, for Saturn takes its cyclic 28-30 years to complete a journey through the twelve houses as well as through the signs. Thus there is a subsidiary cycle, similar to the Saturn return cycle, which starts with each transit over the angles, particularly the Ascendant. One writer, Marc Robertson, even considers the cycles from each conjunction with every planet in the birth chart.

When Saturn enters any house it asks that work is done in relation to the affairs of the house and that lessons are learned in this sphere of experience. Because the angular houses are the strongest in terms of personal activity, these transits provide the more specific opportunities for growth. Saturn in the fourth house brings lessons, responsibilities or work connected with home, family, sense of security or the very stand-point of one's position in life. The transit into the seventh house focuses on close personal relationships and partnership—some people may get happily married, others may have relationship difficulties, but the learning principles behind the manifested events are of the same quality. The transit over the Midheaven and into the tenth house brings lessons in one's externalized position in society (e.g. extra career responsibility, promotion at work or difficulty with the public image). After each of these transits, a 28-30-year cycle, relating to the appropriate angle, will be set in motion, but the cycle that starts with the first house is the most important.

When Saturn crosses the Ascendant there is often a feeling of personal restriction and difficulty, but this is only a reaction to the demands of a new phase of personal development. The most positive approach is to take the opportunity to lay solid foundations for the future—usually the specific requirements are blatantly obvious, but if there is any doubt a little sincere thought and reflection will quickly reveal them. From this point in time the progress of Saturn through the houses in their natural order will allow growth and development in each area of life experience. The first quadrant (houses 1, 2, 3) concentrates on personal development; the second quadrant (houses 4, 5, 6) develops self-expression through the immediate environment, creativity and work; the third quadrant (houses 7, 8, 9) focuses on relationships with other people; the fourth quadrant (houses 10, 11, 12) develops externalized expressions through the wider environment, often correlating with tangible achievement. Transits through the cadent houses represent assimilation (particularly houses 6 and 12) and distribution (particularly houses 3 and 9) preparing for the next phase. This is especially true in the case of the twelfth house, which is the completion not only of the fourth quadrant, but also of the complete Saturn/Ascendant cycle. Saturn transiting the twelfth house is a digesting of a whole period of learning, a gathering together and a preparing for another new beginning.

I believe that it is always appropriate to take a positive and optimistic attitude towards Saturn transits, but it would be unrealistic to suggest that these transits can never be unpleasant. In a birth chart where Saturn has a difficult placing, the transits will be more demanding. Examples of a difficult Saturn might be not only where there are exact squares or quincunxes to personal planets and where Saturn is angular, but also where it is combined with other features in the chart that clash—what I define as the 'qualitative opposition', a useful interpretive concept. In a woman's chart, an exact Saturn square Venus is undermining enough, but if Saturn is angular conjunct the seventh house cusp and yet there are other contrasting indicators that demand relationship involvement (e.g. Libra emphasized and a strong sexuality shown by Scorpio or eighth house), then the tests and lessons of Saturn transits, in such an example, are going to be tougher.

It is useful to consider the circumstances of two different birth charts, one with an 'easy' Saturn and the other with a 'difficult' Saturn. If the latter has an angular Saturn it may very well correlate with a difficult or disciplinarian father, and hence a hard upbringing and unpleasant early years. This will affect the child psychologically, emphasizing the effects of Saturn in his developed character—exaggerated self-discipline and hardness of character, or underconfidence and insecurity. But whatever the tough Saturn lessons may be in the birth chart, demands on the individual will be made at the appointed times when the Saturn transits occur. It is likely that the period up to the Saturn return will be the most difficult, because this is the first cycle of maturity, when trial and error are more relevant than calling on personal experience. Thereafter, if the individual can find and hold on to the narrow pathway of Saturn confrontation, then a disciplined life can produce personal progress. The person with the 'easy' Saturn has more chance of a comfortable life, but if this individual finds self-discipline difficult, and has tried to evade Saturn or has just not bothered to attend to the lessons, then the schoolteacher of the zodiac can still be very strict and harshly exacting.

To ask why there should be such differences in the Saturn experience is to question the philosophical basis of astrology at the deepest level. If one discounts the theory that an easy or difficult birth chart merely represents the random distribution of a biochemical lottery, then it seems that there must be some purpose behind the variations. I dislike the idea of a supreme creator who decides which human beings have easy charts and which have to endure more difficulties in life, because it discounts personal responsibility. I prefer to believe that there is choice involved: that the person (or some inner eternal part of that person—one may call it the soul) chooses the chart, with its 'easy' or 'difficult' Saturn, chooses the parents, the inherited characteristics and the socio-economic environment—indeed the whole package of life potential. Thus, the one person, who almost cannot avoid experiencing the harsher side of Saturn, in some way needed the tests and probably actively chose them, but the reasons for the choice are always obscured from personal consciousness. The other person with the more comfortable chart chose that also—for reasons just as unknowable.

Uranus: Transits of Uranus are easy to pinpoint and apparently easy to interpret as well, for the effect is sudden, disrupting and yet excitingly electrifying. Change, progress and developmental breakthrough are all possible under such a transit and the effects most commonly occur in the visible environment, whether physically or less tangibly. But specific interpretation, verging on prediction, is not so easy because the influence of Uranus is always unexpected. As with all transits, the timing of an event associated with this planet seldom occurs on the precise day when the transit is exact. This phenomena is common to all forecasting and is a result of the complex myriads of combinations, amalgamations, correlations and permutations of the astrological movements that are happening every day and that can shift the neat timing of associated events without our being able to account for it. It is characteristic of Uranus that the actual occurrence relating to the transit is often the very one that was not on the list of possibilities. With hindsight, the correlation is obvious, but the best attitude to take before the transit is always to expect the unexpected.

The nature of change itself needs to be considered. Anyone who is interested in psychology, serious astrology or the motivations of human beings has an interest in change. Indeed, anyone who wants to improve his position in life in any way—job, money, relationship, home—is seeking change. The paradox is that most people are apprehensive about the very process they seek and, however alluring the new pastures may be, there seems to be safety and comfort in existing circumstances, in the tried and trusted methods that have previously enabled them to cope adequately with life and its requirements. There is a risk that the change may not be an improvement—'better the devil you know', and 'out of the frying pan into the fire', say the voices of caution and inertia. Any change is likely to be inconvenient at the time, even if it is from worse to better, and the attraction of short-term comfort is often the option taken.

These are the circumstances that bring a glint to the eye of Uranus, the awakener. It is almost as though the very purpose of a Uranus transit is to shake up the complacency of the existing order and force progress and development on to a slack-bellied populace. To someone who is not even looking out for the unexpected, Uranus acts with suddenness and speed and the more fixed are the sets of behaviour patterns, the more disruptive are the changes which must come about. The injured response 'But that's the way we've always done it' brings out the angry explosiveness of marauding Uranus—the sacred cow is a red rag to the bull.

Thus any transit will provide the opportunity to cast away that which has become outgrown, outmoded and over-used. The moment is available when breakthrough can be achieved. Fore-knowledge of such a transit enables the individual to plan and prepare for change, even if he is not sure in what guise it will occur, and often an electrified anticipation accompanies the build-up. The very nature of the effect of this transit generates a fully-wound tautness that hastens the outcome. An earthy fixed sign type of person can be expected to find Uranus disquietingly unsettling, but even a Uranian birth chart character is unlikely to take the transit peacefully in his stride. Indeed, the true benefits would be lost if it were possible to achieve a radical change of circumstances, attitude or emotional quality as simply as moving the hands of a clock from twelve to six. The tension and highly strung energy make the experience all the more vivid and memorable, often spilling over into the material environment so that the very fabric and structure of a person's life is changed.

The fact that Uranus, by its very nature, needs to express its influence in a more tangible form in the outer world means that its transits are often uncomfortably disrupting. It is possible to internalize the effects to some extent, but this subjective focus is less easy to achieve than with other transiting planets.

More specifically, but subsidiary to the broad interpretive considerations, are the variations of change that may occur. The experience may not necessarily be change *of*—job, home or relationship, for example—but it can equally validly be change *to* or change *in* whatever is indicated by the transit. The employee of a company may well move to another organization when Uranus transits his Midheaven, but there are numerous other options. He may move into a completely different field of work, or he may just change departments; a new boss may disrupt his working life or he may have the opportunity to apply revolutionary new techniques to existing systems. If he is an ambitious executive, he may come to accept that he has reached his ceiling within the company and change his attitude to life accordingly. Or, remembering the un-expected nature of the transit, his mother may remarry a famous politician who makes her a director of his electronics leisure company and she gives her son a full-sized Space Invaders machine for his living room. (That would change his life!)

Uranus takes about seven years to transit through an average sized house in the birth chart and in a satisfactorily long life will bring its progressive and inventive energy to all areas of experience as defined by each one of the houses. Change and disturbance may accompany the period of transit, but where no other factors are taken into consideration, the changes can easily be evolutionary rather than revolutionary. The opportunity is for progress, development and new possibilities as the awakener's magic wand sweeps around the complete spectrum of life.

Neptune: Neptune dissolves and rarifies all that it contacts. Its intangible qualities are able to inspire and refine if the individual will allow this to happen; but it can just as easily confuse reality and entice a person to lethargic escape on the banks of the river of forgetfulness. Because of its illusory qualities, Neptune is not easy to handle when it is making an important transit—indeed the very idea of trying to 'handle' it is ill-advised, for that implies grasping the situation firmly and taking concrete action. Neptune encourages us to do just the opposite, to let go and achieve results by 'non-doing'.

In 84 years, a notional lifetime, Neptune will have passed through half the houses in the birth chart, but the effect of its progress is so mystical and fog-enshrouded that the many years spent in one house may not seem to correlate with any obvious results. This exemplifies the mysterious paradox of Neptune—the more one searches for tangible effects, the more labyrinthine the swirls of mist become; but as soon as one lets go and allows the vision to form itself, then the benediction will descend. Thus, the house where Neptune is transiting will be the area of life where surrender is necessary and where inspiration and spiritual nourish-ment can be found.

Although so much of the influence that Neptune brings is beyond our rational grasp, it is wrong to assume that the only reaction recommended is to remain passive. Certainly too much active 'doing' during the period of a Neptune transit will result in confusion, evaporation and false scents; but the other extreme of total inactivity allows the insidious aspect of the planet's influence to seep into the individual's life and create deterioration and wasting away. Neptune often brings the need for escape and the temptation is to take the easy routes, such as subsiding into non-stop daydreaming or the self-destructive routes of drug and alcohol abuse. More positive escape can be found in musical appreciation, which is intangible and inactive but is also psychically enriching when the inspired work of a great composer pervades the atmosphere. The actual creation or playing of music is even better, but that is not so available for everyone. Meditative activity is a perfect example of active passivity and one should remember that it is not necessary to wear a turban and sit cross-legged on the floor to meditate. Meditation is an attitude of mind, allowing oneself to be open to more refined energies, to draw them in and to use them as a positive inspiration. A walk in the park, talking silently to nature and the trees or standing at the sea shore can be just as much of a meditation as sitting in an ashram. The same process can be achieved at any time or place, from bus queue to lavatory seat.

A person will also be susceptible to deception, illusion and glamour when Neptune is transiting and it is here that the planet is at its most seductive. The idea, the opportunity or the promise of success and fame beckons enticingly and fascination with that glamorous illusion obscures reality. Thus, it becomes crucial that some form of land-anchor is retained so that however high the inflations fly, contact is still retained with the physical world. Association with films, show business, music, publicity and scandal are all possible when Neptune is active in a chart, but the dividing line between the positive and negative sides of many such associations is almost indefinable. An actress who has a wonderful chance for her first major screen role might have Neptune transiting her natal Sun. Whether the opportunity turns out to be as beneficial as she had hoped, whether her dreams were pie in the sky or whether she is used as a glamorous puppet by the moguls, her contract being revealed as a profitless shackle, depends either on the helpfulness of other aspects operative at the time (Saturn would be especially useful) or on her intelligence, consciousness and ability to allow the positive effects of the transit to manifest. The way in which Neptune is placed in the natal chart will also indicate how easy or difficult the latter will be.

The actress is an example showing the more material aspects of glamour and fantasy. Because Neptune brings other-worldly influences it associates strongly with religious experience and can allow an individual to discover how to sacrifice and surrender elements of his life to a more refined and spiritual cause. But the temptations for escape and the glamours that exist in the world of religion and spirituality are even more subtly seductive and insidiously dangerous than material glamours—there are many gurus, groups and -isms that will be only too delighted to join with Neptune and manipulate these weaknesses.

The key to understanding and interpreting Neptune transits is that unless there is some attunement to a higher consciousness, a sutratma-like connecting thread, then deception, uncertainties and confusion will take over and manifest in the scandals, frauds, daydreaming or drug-taking typical of the lowest Neptunian denominator. The higher attunement draws one away from the material world and brings the opportunity to experience the meaning and importance of spiritual awareness. The acquisition of this refined sensitivity will surely lead to a more delicate perception of the subtler aspects of life, to a responsive *sympathique* with one's fellow beings or to inspired creative expression; but this can only be achieved if the land-anchor, the earthing wire, is connected. This is not necessarily to create a material attitude to whatever is happening under the transit, but to prevent the person from floating away into the ephemeral pink clouds that always adorn the Neptunian environment.

Pluto: The transits of Pluto are among the most powerful of astrological influences and the principle behind them is always one of potential transformation. The symbol of the phoenix epitomizes this—the mythological bird would end its life by putting itself into the fire at Heliopolis, but it was always reborn, rising again out of the ashes. So it is with transits of Pluto—being consumed by fire may not be comfortable, but there is each time rebirth and renewal to a new plane of experience.

The myths of the gods of the underworld help us to understand the nature of this planet's transits. There is a certain duality in many of these stories, evil and fearsome images joined with positive, redeeming experiences. There is also always a descent into the infernal regions. In Greek mythology, the god is known as both Hades and Pluto. As Hades he was feared and hated by the other gods as well as by men; as Pluto (also his Roman name) he was the god of riches and was venerated as the receiver of buried treasure.

Also, it was he who made the crops grow from deep within the earth. Hades took his wife Persephone after a secret agreement with Zeus by abducting her while she was picking narcissus daffodils and taking her to his underground kingdom. Her broken-hearted mother, Demeter, cast famine on the earth and made the soil sterile to force the other gods to bring her daughter back. But before Persephone left the underworld Hades enticed her to eat a pomegranate seed, a symbol of indissoluble marriage, and thus he made her his wife for ever. Zeus allowed a compromise: the girl should be allowed to spend part of each year in the upper world in her other aspect, Kore. The four months spent in the underworld symbolize the time the seeds spend in the ground, while the remaining eight months represent the time of fruitfulness. Not only did Hades/Pluto spend most of his time deep in his underground kingdom, but if he decided to visit the upper world, he also had a helmet which made him invisible. Astrologically, by transit, Pluto's influence indeed operates at the deepest of levels and the effects are felt within the psyche much more intensely than they are manifested outside. The material results of a Pluto transit often take some time to occur, in the same way as the effects of an underground explosion may not be immediately obvious on the surface.

The deity of the Babylonian underworld was a fearsome goddess, Allatu, also known as Ereshkigal. This was the sister of Ishtar, the goddess of love and war, who in different ways was almost more formidable than the hell-queen sibling herself. Ishtar's war chariot was drawn by seven lions and she was terrifying in battle, but she treated her many lovers almost as harshly as her enemies. Sacred prostitution formed part of her cult and her rites were celebrated with uninhibited licentiousness. If her lovers were animals they became weakened and prone to capture or subjugation by men. After coupling with humans she would usually change them into animals—a shepherd into a wolf to be chased away or a gardener into a bat, flitting in the darkness. Even her lovers among the gods suffered.

There was, however, one lover whom she mourned—Tammuz, the young god of nature who each year came to life and then died again. It was for Tammuz that she journeyed to the underworld in the hope that she could resurrect him and make him her consort. There were seven gates to the Babylonian land of the dead and at each one she was progressively stripped of all adornment and clothing until she was naked in front of her sister Allatu. They fought and Allatu made Ishtar her prisoner. She was locked up, had the sixty maladies released upon her or was impaled on a peg or hook—the stories vary. But if Ishtar remained in the lower world, all generation amongst living creatures would cease and thus the great god Ea had to rescue her. He did this by creating a man whom he sent to Allatu, a man who pleased her as much as Ishtar displeased her. Some accounts suggest he was a strong and forceful lover, others tell of an androgynous being or a man with feminine qualities. The earlier Sumerian version of the myth tells how Enki, the god of waters and of wisdom, rescued the goddess by creating two little mourners from the dirt under his fingernails. They were androgynous almost in the sense of being in a state of undifferentiated sexuality, pre-sexual in their simplicity. Ishtar was sprinkled with the water of life and released.

So much of what is in these powerful myths reflects the nature of the transits of the planet Pluto. Pain or violence may precede the new growth and regeneration. This is reflected in the fact that Ishtar was goddess of war as well as of love and often she consumed her lovers. Similarly, virginal Kore was forced into her coupling with Hades. Both Tammuz and Persephone/Kore symbolize the eternal cycle of death and rebirth—the seed must lie dormant in the cold barren earth, while nature mourns, before there can be new growth and rejoicing in the harvest. Hades/Pluto may rule the dead, but he also gives mineral wealth and causes the crops to grow by pushing them up through the ground. If Persephone/Kore and Tammuz remain in the underworld, nothing grows; if Ishtar is a tortured prisoner of Alluta, living beings can no longer make love and procreate. Descent into the darkness is the only way to redeem that which has been lost or has died and it may be no easy journey, but this is what the transits of Pluto offer or even demand. Like the powerful Ishtar, we may have to be stripped bare, to lose our psychological clothing—fineries, affectations, habits and defences —so that we can be born again from our nakedness.

There will be few major Pluto transits in an individual's life. Taking conjunctions, oppositions and squares as a group, it is most unlikely that there will be more than two of these aspects made to any one planet in the natal chart in a lifetime. Because Pluto moves slowly and has lengthy and frequent periods retrograde, the span of undulating effect may last from one to three years, so when the transits do occur they must be viewed as highly significant. As with Uranus, change is a factor, but here it is deep inner change, which may take time to show outside. Pluto works on psychological factors of great importance to the individual's development and brings them to the surface or to personal consciousness. If this process is resisted, then it can be inordinately disagreeable; but if the need for transformation is recognized, if there is a degree of letting go (for resistances will surely be broken as violently as Kore was abducted), then the process of the transit will be not only bearable, but also a journey of adventure. One of the most positive ways of channelling and containing Pluto's energy is to start some sort of psychotherapeutic work—analysis, group psychotherapy or a disciplined programme of self-investigation. As in the myths, Pluto can indeed be associated with actual physical death, perhaps of a parent or someone close, but it is more appropriately the death of an old inner attitude whose presence was standing in the way of a new birth.

In the Sumerian myth, the key to the release of the goddess is the dirt under Enki's fingernails. It is an insignificant, unnoticeable amount of matter, which nevertheless can be used with considerable creative power. In the myths of creation, the first being is created from the slime or dust—'And the Lord God formed a man of the dust of the ground and breathed into his nostrils the breath of life' (Genesis). In alchemy, the whole process towards the philosopher's stone and towards gold starts with *prima materia*, primal matter. Pluto, by transit, can work on that base material and release tremendous power from it, as in the process of splitting the atom or like a supreme being creating a new man. Pluto, as it were, takes the eliminated waste material, creates heat in the middle of the compost heap and then transforms it into the fertilizer that can feed new life.

New and Full Moons
When transiting Sun and transiting Moon are conjunct it is said to be a new Moon; when they are in opposition it is a full Moon. Conjunctions and oppositions occur when two bodies are on the same degree of zodiacal longitude, but if the Sun and Moon are also on the same degree of zodiacal latitude or of declination (distance above or below the celestial equator), then an eclipse occurs. The new Moon becomes a solar eclipse as the disc of the Moon obscures the Sun and, the full Moon becomes a lunar eclipse as the Earth's shadow falls on the Moon and obscures or darkens it. Any detailed forecasting work should include reference to new and full Moons,

but because they are traditionally considered more as a tool for mundane astrology they seem to be less commonly used in personal work.

In mundane astrology, new and full Moons, especially eclipses, have always been important phenomena. The chart of the precise moment of a solar eclipse, for example, is used as a mundane indicator and any significant correspondences and mutual aspects with the charts of nations and world leaders would be interpreted accordingly. An individual's chart can also be compared with the eclipse chart (in a similar manner to some of the interpretative methods for solar and lunar returns), but this is linking an ordinary individual very much with the collective and as a forecasting method it does not seem as appropriate as it is for Popes, Presidents and Prime Ministers, who have a greater involvement and influence on the collective. There is also evidence to suggest that the eclipse is stronger for the people and countries where it is visible, but again this is more relevant in mundane than individual astrology. (A lunar eclipse is visible to everyone on that half of the Earth which is turned towards the Moon. A solar eclipse is visible only to a person who is in the eclipse path, which is of variable length, but only about seventy miles wide.)

Interpretation: Traditional astrology places much more emphasis on eclipses than on new and full Moons and, in the past, they were considered to be exclusively 'malefic influences'. I prefer the more contemporary attitudes to interpretation, which suggest that any new or full Moon, eclipse or not, will activate that part of the chart where it falls. Activation can be defined as a sharp focus which boosts or energizes, sometimes providing a positive potential, but often demanding extra action and creating a flurry of activity. The influence has a certain positive neutrality and should be viewed as drawing to the surface whatever the contact in the natal chart means. For example, if an eclipse falls on the indulgently aspected Jupiter in the second house, an exaggerated money crisis is likely to follow. The inherent natal chart tendency to enjoy overspending would result in a greater extravagance and a correspondingly heavier retribution.

The conjunction is the most important aspect to consider when evaluating full and new Moons, followed by the opposition. Indeed, in the case of a full Moon, the Sun-Moon opposition will automatically both conjunct and oppose any sensitive natal degree at the same time. I recommend small orbs, say within two degrees. Other aspects can be considered also, but they are very much subsidiary to the conjunction. The house position is relevant, but where a natal planet is conjuncted its house will automatically be taken into account in the interpretation.

The affairs of the house in which the new or full Moon falls, even if no natal planet is aspected, may sometimes be highlighted, but the effect is not strong. In the case of a full Moon, the house polarity is emphasized and this will be especially noticeable if it occurs conjunct the angles. For example, a working mother with a young child experienced a full Moon on the MC/IC axis. She was completely dependent on a daily child-minder so that she could do her job, but for the few weeks after the full Moon there was a period of problems with unreliable helpers, sickness and difficulty in employing a suitable person. This directly affected the home/career axis of the fourth and tenth houses.

Which is stronger, the new Moon or the full? Astronomically, at the full Moon the Earth is directly between the two major bodies in the solar system, as if suspended on a taut line of energy stretching from one to the other. That this power can be used positively or negatively is seen in various ways. It is said that there are greater disturbances and restlessness in mental hospitals at the time of the full Moon and in America certain police precincts have been known to increase the duty roster at this time. But it is also when group meditations are supposed to be particularly effective, and many esotericists try and tune in individually with the thousands of other people doing likewise all over the world when the Moon is full. Passover always occurs on the day of the first full Moon after the vernal equinox and Easter, the starting point for the annual Christian calendar, is the Sunday after that same full Moon.

A new Moon, on the other hand, is a concentration of energy on one degree of the zodiac, and a Solar eclipse is an awsomely dramatic occurrence where it is total—even to 'civilized' man. It is small wonder that ancient man, who still respected the gods, treated the event as highly significant and ominous—the Sun, the Lord and Giver of Life, disappears for a terrifying few minutes. Today we can experience vicariously something of this feeling when animals panic as the Sun is totally eclipsed. In primitive religions, people give thanks when the new Moon starts to grow after its apparent absence and popular superstitions say that it is lucky to see that first delicate crescent Moon undistorted by glass.

We should make a wish at this time and turn over the money in our pockets. I have not examined a large enough number of cases for statistical reliability, but from my own experience the full Moon is the stronger. (98 per cent of all werewolves agree with this!)

Symbolically, the new Moon is a time of new beginnings, of conception and of planting new seeds and this is a useful concept to take into account when interpreting. The Moon's first quarter is a time of growing, of flexing muscles and stretching wings. It is a time when the first challenges are experienced. Thus the full Moon, after the waxing phase, can be seen as a time of peak power and productivity, a culmination of achievement. The third quarter, in the waning phase, is a time of feeding on the harvest, be it sparse or abundant, and it is when an introversion begins before the next new beginning occurs again. Thus, if there is any difference between the strength and type of effect of a new or full Moon, the former tends to offer a potential for a new start of some sort, while the latter presents a powerful outflow of energy.

Timing: The basic rule for the timing of activity associated with new and full Moons is that the effects will occur usually in the two weeks up to the next Sun-Moon conjunction or opposition and sometimes later, during the complete lunar month itself. Often the activity will appear to extend over a period of several months. This is because the numerical degree of the full or new Moon in a certain sign will change only gradually (decreasing) as it moves on from sign to sign each month. Thus, a new Moon separating from the conjunction of Mars conjunct Uranus in the birth chart one month will very likely to be square the natal conjunction three months later. The new Moon six months later may even be within orbs of the opposition and all the intervening new Moons will have made minor or softer aspects each month. In this example, the unpredictably volatile natal aspect would have been strongly activated, resulting in a highly energized period that could produce anything from an exciting new breakthrough to a series of mishaps or accidents. As in all forecasting, it depends on how Mars and Uranus fit into the rest of the birth chart and what degree of consciousness and personal responsibility the individual has. The progressions and transits must also be taken into account. The example given would be more likely to correlate with activity only of irritant quality and of transitory importance if no major progression or transits were in effect. But if the series of new Moons occurred when Uranus was transiting over the Ascendant and progressed Sun was conjunct Saturn, then a period of major importance and change could be forecast. The new Moon activity would certainly sharpen the other influences, but in practice it would be difficult to differentiate between the effects of the new Moons and the transits and progressions.

For the record, traditional astrology suggests that, although most eclipses (and to a lesser extent, presumably, new and full Moons) are unfavourable in their influence, they can bring good results when the other transits and the progressions are favourable. It is said that the effect of an eclipse may not be felt until years later, when another planet, usually Mars or Saturn, transits the degree. I am doubtful about this. If the eclipse falls on the Ascendant and nothing apparently happens, Mars or Saturn conjunct the Ascendant years later, producing a noticeable effect, has nothing to do with the eclipse. If the eclipse does not aspect anything in the birth chart, when Mars or Saturn transits that degree the astrological circumstances will be the same for every individual in the world, if there is any validity in this approach. The relevance to mundane astrology seems more appropriate.

Finally, new and full Moons can often act as trigger points for activity associated with other broader progressions and transits in force at the time. When this occurs it may seem that the new or full Moon is responsible for a surprising amount of activity, whereas it is the other astrological significators that have the more important correlation. When the other progressions and transits are quiet and inactive, full and new Moons will be marked by relatively inconsequential effects which, although receiving a lot of attention and energy at the time, are nevertheless short-lived in their importance.

5.
APPROACHES
TO INTERPRETATION

Understanding the meaning of a given progression or transit as it applies to a particular birth chart is only one part of the complete exercise of forecasting. Each influence needs to be considered in relation to the others operating at the same time, but there are also a number of broader interpretative factors that must be discussed as well. These miscellanea are covered first in this chapter and are then followed by more practical considerations. There are so many different astrological influences operating at any one time, each with different strength and importance and each extending over varying periods, that it is vital to develop an efficient method of handling the mass of information available.

Throughout this book the importance of the natal chart has been emphasized. If a new client comes to an astrologer wanting only to have progressions and transits updated for the coming year or two, I recommend giving at least a short summary interpretation of the birth chart before embarking on the forecasting, whether their previous astrologer is known and trusted or not. Whatever may be happening in a chart by progression or transit must always be referred back to the natal pattern to check what is suggested or promised by the birth chart. What may appear to be highly favour-able progressions and transits will be substantially restrained by a birth chart that has an inbuilt austerity and lack of ease. Similarly, where the indicators appear to suggest a concentration of un-pleasantness, in a more harmonious birth chart the effects may quite probably be merely annoying, but quite tolerable.

Thus, every progression and transit will have its own individual meaning in each birth chart. Both the natal planet and, to a lesser extent the moving planet must be considered by its sign placing in the birth chart to determine the quality of the planetary energy, by its house placing to determine the focus of its energy and, most importantly, by aspect to discover the dynamic modifications of the energy. For example, Neptune transiting square Mercury in Pisces would emphasize a confused or a psychic mentality, but if Mercury is in Virgo the transit would either confuse or inspire an orderly mind. If Mercury is in the twelfth house, an inner contemplative tendency would be exaggerated, whereas a man with a third-house Mercury might have his writing and conversational interests either uplifted or evaporated. Natal aspects to Mercury are also likely to be relevant. Reference to houses ruled will also help to indicate how the transit may take effect. As discussed in previous chapters, the house position of the moving planet (and to a lesser extent its sign) will also be relevant. With practice and experience these steps are taken automatically, but it is important to draw attention to them.

More obvious is the importance of examining all the moving factors in a chart over the period in question before attempting any forecasting for that period. It is an ever-present temptation to concentrate on (or even to become mesmerized by) one or two transits, and sometimes progressions, that may be operative. These will usually be either the obvious indicators, the easy ones to spot or the exciting ones, which are often the easiest to interpret. In this context I am referring to exciting influences in the eyes of the astrologer rather than the friend or client. Many are the times that an amateur astrologer has gleefully pointed out that in a few months time Saturn or Pluto will transit over Sun, Moon or Venus. The astrologer is oblivious to the cry for help expressed by the proffering of a scruffy photocopy of a chart drawn up years ago and omits to give a considered interpretation of this transit, combined with the other influences, which could correlate with highly significant events in that person's life.

Even a more responsible astrologer may be tempted by some dazzling transits and may be unwittingly lured by what I call the power trap to show off his skills, forecast events and tell the other person what to do. He presumes to play at being God for a while, in the guise of saviour and helper. Firstly, in practical terms, all the transits and progressions must be examined before any interpretation can be put together. For example, transiting Saturn conjunct the Sun will have very different meanings if at the same time either progressed Venus is conjunct Uranus, or progressed Mars conjunct Pluto, or progressed Sun conjunct Jupiter. Secondly, in terms of presentation, the balance between advice and help and between prediction, forecast and mere description of the influences needs to be considered. Individuals' own reality and personal objectives must be respected; their life path is where they are travelling at any given time and the odds are that it will be a different path to the astrologer's. C. G. Jung, speaking of the relationship between analytical psychologist and patient, was even more categoric: 'The greatest mistake an analyst can make is to assume that his patient has a psychology similar to his own.'

In respecting a person's reality and needs it is often difficult to know how much advice to give, especially when a distraught client asks 'What shall I do?' or 'Tell me what is going to happen'. Prediction feeds a suggestible mind and many people will go out of their way to fulfil the astrologer's prophecy. And when they return to praise the astrologer and announce that it all came true as predicted, they are offering back an even more dangerous food, which sustains the God-playing power fantasy within the astrologer. This collusion is all too common and a trap that is so easy to fall into, but it makes no healthy contribution to either person, nor to any other people with whom the two come into contact. Often a person will not take the advice given, for there are times when the psyche or the soul knows that it needs an apparently disastrous episode in order to experience the pit, or one might even go so far as to say the power of evil itself, so that the ego is pulled out of its irresponsible attitude and pushed towards maturity. Self-satisfied complacency can only be brought to consciousness by drastic experience.

Students often ask how much detail they should go into when attempting forecasting. In the initial stages it is advisable to examine only the conjunctions, squares and oppositions of the progressed Sun, Mercury, Venus and Mars and of transiting Pluto, Neptune, Uranus and Saturn. Conjunctions of the progressed Moon should also be included and, in charts where the degrees of the natal angles can be trusted, the progressed Ascendant and Midheaven also. As experience is gained through practice, more detail can be introduced—quincunxes, sextiles, trines and the 45° aspects. All aspects of the progressed Moon and the transits of Jupiter can be added; so can full and new Moons and solar arc directions and any preferred other techniques (see chapter 8). It is a case of individual taste and each astrologer will develop a style and approach that suits him or her. Personally, I find a lot of detail may be confusing rather than enlightening and if anyone was to use all the available forecasting techniques in their fullest expression, the only possible prediction the astrologer could make from his own chart would be: 'You are going to spend the whole of the next year at your desk working with books of tables and a calculator—even longer if you attempt to work on anyone else's chart'. I prefer astrology to be contributory and subsidiary to the rest of life, not the other way round.

The question of how much detail obviously also depends on the person requesting astrological advice. Many clients do not want detailed monthly or weekly forecasts and prefer to know the broad trends only. These people will tend to be more interested in working with their understanding of the natal chart and its life unfoldment, allowing the more transient monthly and weekly influences to be experienced spontaneously in their feelings and in daily life. Other clients seek a greater degree of guidance and need advance information and outside confirmation of all life's ephemeral happenings. The danger with this latter individual is that astrology (and the astrologer) may take over the running of the life and personal responsibility disappears, stunting the chance for psychological growth. The former individual, however, may miss out on using astrology to its fullest advantage as an aid to fulfilled and successful living, so it is important to maintain as sensible a balance in astrological future-watching as in anything else. Where any extreme exists there will always be an unconscious opposite extreme providing the balance; whatever is unconscious can manipulate its host unknown, causing complex difficulties in personal life and entangling all relationships with involuntary projections. So the central balance point, the middle way, implies a healthy degree of consciousness of both extremes and from this vantage point the astrologer can choose the techniques, the detail and the approach to clients that genuinely suits him—and not be inhibited about changing as he evolves as a person and increases his knowledge of astrology and other relevant subjects.

Strength of Aspects: It is not possible to lay down rules about the strength of aspects, for each case must be considered individually in each different natal chart. For example, although the Sun is always an important indicator, usually the most important, in a chart where the Sun is in Pisces in the twelfth house and Mars is angular rising in Aries, progressed Mars would have a more extroverted effect than the progressed Sun in many instances and might apparently be stronger.

In general terms, aspects are stronger when closer to exactness. Theoretically, applying aspects are stronger than separating, but I am not entirely convinced of this practice. There is usually a greater tension as the aspect moves towards its exact degree, but often the result of the contact, whether it is in terms of physical events, emotional experiences or internalized understanding, occurs after the peak, during the separating phase. The use of the word strength in this context may be too simplistic, but it does emphasize the weakness of categoric statements in astrology. Progressed aspects to natal planets are stronger than progressed to progressed and than directions, in my experience. It is impossible to say whether progressions are stronger than transits and the only answer is that it depends on the circumstances. If pressed, I would say that a progression is possibly more important because of its long slow period of influence. Certainly progressed Sun conjunct Saturn would be felt more strongly than a simultaneous Jupiter transit over Venus angular on the Ascendant, but Jupiter would allow the experience of Saturn's dark clouds to have its silver linings and perhaps benefits would accrue from the enforced discipline of the Saturn contact. However, if progressed Sun was conjunct Jupiter at the same time as strong Saturn activity by transit, the relative strengths are debatable. The progression would help a Saturn return or Saturn conjunct Ascendant to be an especially positive start of a new cycle; but if Saturn was transiting Mars or Venus, for example, then frustrations and difficulties would have to be experienced in order to realize Jupiter's opportunities and the transiting influence might well feel stronger to that individual.

Any station, progressed or transiting, will always be strong, but even here one should be careful not to confuse length of influence with strength. A station of progressed Mars would be within a 1° orb of aspect for around twenty-five years and therefore almost becomes part of the birth chart. Transiting stations have particular additional strength when they contact sensitive points in the birth chart, but a retrograde transit generally has no different an effect than a direct transit. Usually three (and very occasionally five) transits are made when a planet goes retrograde and, depending on the timing, it will mean an extended period of influence relating to the interaction of the moving planet and the natal contact. However, it is sometimes possible to differentiate between the three —the first (direct) contact is the preparation, the second (retrograde) is the actualization and the third (direct) is the outcome.

Sometimes a station will not quite reach a sensitive point in the birth chart. Because a station does produce a concentration of that planet's energy, it is legitimate to extend the orbs normally used and in this example some effect might be felt three or even four degrees away. If Uranus was the planet in question, such a stationary transit might serve as some sort of advance warning, a smoke signal on a distant hill, of what the actual transit would bring in terms of unexpected change some months later.

It is possible and legitimate to use contacts of transiting planets to progressed planets in carrying out forecasting work. Many people find such aspects satisfactorily significant, but this is not my personal experience. If they are used, I recommend treating them as subsidiary to other transits and to progressions.

Orbs: The size of orbs to use in forecasting work is a personal matter, but they will certainly be smaller than their acceptable equivalents in the natal chart. In general terms, I suggest using one degree applying and one degree separating, but it would be foolish to suggest that the influence suddenly stops when the moving planet reaches one degree and one minute away from exact. It depends on the circumstances in each case and where three (or even five) transits are involved, as with retrograde motion, the whole period will be one of undulating influence of the nature of the transiting planet. As I said in my first book in this series,* orbs can be likened to the sound of a gong as it dies away—it depends on the strength of the beat, the sensitivity of the ear, the amount of background noise and the acoustics of the environment. Thus it is perfectly valid to watch for effects from a transit up to around two degrees before and after exactitude.

Because the movement of progressed planets is generally slower and steadier, slightly tighter orbs may be taken. For example a solar progression is usually in effect for about a year to eighteen months, which correlate with movement of approximately 1°-1½°. Thus many people favour orbs for progressions of half a degree either side or one degree applying and half a degree separating. Stephen Arroyo, in his excellent book *Astrology, Karma and Transformation*, suggests orbs of time for the progressed Moon. Although this is technically no different from orbs of longitude, it is a particularly useful concept. It draws our thinking away from rigid orbs and encourages an attitude of applying the progressions to

_____
* *How to Interpret a Birth Chart* (Aquarian Press, 1981).

practical aspects of real life, with a certain flexibility if necessary. It can also be applied with equal validity to progressions other than the Moon.

Handling the Information: Although I have recommended students to start forecasting by using only the major aspects of the important planetary indicators, it is obviously preferable to use as much information as can be digested, since it is all relevant, but with varying strength of influence. The Faculty of Astrological Studies publishes a useful progression worksheet, which allows a lot of information to be expressed succinctly and understandably in one place and many Faculty Diploma holders find this form a boon when they are drawing together all the forecasting information they like to use. It is also an excellent discipline when one is starting to work with detailed forecasting. After experience has been gained, people who dislike forms (myself included), may prefer to develop their own systems and, as an example of how to use a plain sheet of paper and to make it suit one's own needs, I have also included an example of my own method.

Whatever type of display is used on paper, the preparatory work must be done first. Once the noon date or midnight date has been found, the progressed day in the ephemeris can be found for the year under review. Then the information is put down on paper. I use an ordinary sheet of A4 paper, ruled into about five columns. In the first column I put my astrological notes on the natal chart, in blue. In the second column, in green, I list all the progressed and transiting aspects of planets and angles in order of importance and broadly by speed of movement. Thus, the slow moving progressions appear first, starting with the Sun, followed by Mercury, Venus, Mars, Ascendant and Midheaven. (Although progressed Mars moves the most slowly, this is a convenient order since it follows the ephemeris.) Next come directions; and for convenience, these usually occur in their order around the chart. Having worked out the solar arc, I set it on dividers and apply it to each planet in turn. The point of the dividers enables me to see the aspects more easily. The transiting aspects are inserted in order—Pluto, Neptune, Uranus, Saturn and Jupiter. Finally, the aspects of the progressed Moon are inserted; this is done at the end not because the Moon is considered less important, but because it involves going back to the ephemeris for the year of birth and making calculations for the intermediate positions. The Moon's daily

motion, divided by twelve, gives the progressed motion per month
and the twelve monthly positions can easily be noted (see example
on page 46). For broad forecasting, divide the Moon's daily
motion by four and use quarterly progressed positions for the year
under review.

Once this information is recorded, it is a simple matter to
transcribe it into its order in time, while still retaining its broad
order of importance. Thus the final columns show at a glance, in
black, the important long-acting progressions and transits, first for
the year and then the faster-acting transits and the progressed
Moon by month. An example of Prince Charles' data is given on
page 133 (Figure 10) and Princess Diana's on page 124 (Figure 7).

The Faculty's No. 3 Progressions Worksheet provides many ad-
vantages over the Freeman 'one sheet' method. An example is
given on page 128 (Figure 8). The information in the top left-hand
corner box is straightforward and it allows for converse progressions and for the two methods of calculating the progressed angles.
The MCC (Midheaven constant) is a third method of progressing
the angles (explained on the form), which has the advantage of
needing to be calculated only once for charts where progressions
are to be carried out regularly; but if one is using solar arc directions
the solar arc has to be calculated anyway. Below the basic information box is a column for listing natal planets in numerical order,
making it much easier to spot the aspects, which are inserted in
another column provided. There are spaces for positions by month
of the progressed Moon, transits and full and new Moons and
sections for directions, mid-points and comments. This worksheet
is excellent for detailed work on any given year and gives due
prominence to the progressed Moon, but it is not so convenient if
five years' broad trends are being examined. Nor is the information
listed in order of length of influence, broad importance and by
timing, as with the 'one sheet' method; but it is easy enough to see
the information in order of importance for those people who do not
like the chore of transcribing, which is necessary on my own 'one
sheet' method. However, these two methods are useful examples
and will assist in developing a personal method if required by the
reader.

6.
INTERPRETING
THE INFORMATION

As has been emphasized frequently in this book, interpretation of any moving planetary contact can only be validly made with reference to the birth chart itself. Not only are there different ways in which any contact may manifest itself in practice, but also the two planets involved will have their text book meanings modified by their individual birth chart positions. Thus the interpretations given in the following pages are suggested examples only, taken out of context, and must be treated as such. Reference to the more general interpretive comments earlier in the book is recommended.

Note: Each of the following paragraphs refers to contact between two planets. The word 'and' (e.g. Sun and Venus) refers to all aspects made by Sun to natal Venus and Venus to natal Sun. The word 'to' (e.g. Mars to Pluto) refers only to aspects made by Mars to natal Pluto. Aspects of Pluto to natal Mars are covered in a later paragraph.

The Sun—Progressions and Directions
—First refer to Chapter 3, page 47.
—Modify interpretations in respect of sign, house, aspects and rulerships in the birth chart.
—Likely time period for aspects made by progressed Sun is one to two years.

Sun to Sun: (Possible aspects: semi-sextile, semi-square, sextile and, late in life, square.) A period of potential personal integration or testing. Natal house, sign and aspect capabilities can be realized. Will and life force is energized.

Sun and Moon: Sun conjunct Moon and Sun conjunct progressed Moon (progressed new Moon) both indicate a background opportunity for new beginnings or the start of new personal cycles.

The opposition or the progressed full Moon may be stressful, but it is potentially a time of great productivity. All the possible aspects imply contact between the masculine and the feminine, either in symbolic inner integration or in the outer physical world. There is focus on the emotions; affairs of the Moon's house or house ruled may be involved.

Sun and Mercury: (Limited range of aspects possible.) Stimulates mental and communicative activity. This may be connected with writing, talking, teaching, learning, reading, commercial matters, transportation or travel. Consideration must be given to the houses ruled by Mercury and its placement.

Sun and Venus: (Limited range of aspects possible.) Matters associated with close personal relationships are emphasized, especially if Venus rules seventh or eighth house. Artistic pursuits and social activities are desired or enjoyed, but the less harmonious aspects may stimulate extravagance and indulgence. Since these two planets are never more than 48° apart in the birth chart, a progression of Sun conjunct Venus or Venus conjunct Sun is likely in most lifetimes and this is usually an indicator of an important relationship, unless it happens too early in life.

Sun and Mars: A period of augmented energy and activity. This can be very constructive if the energies are able to be channelled, but impulsiveness, anger and passion can be aroused, which may result in rash behaviour. Independence and assertiveness are stimulated. Overstrain is possible—check Mars in the birth chart.

Sun to Jupiter: A period of opportunity, enjoyment and expansiveness, often success and achievement, particularly in the case of the conjunction. Long distance travel is often experienced. Stimulation of or contact with philosophical or religious affairs is possible. Depending on the natal placing, extravagance, over-indulgence and exhaustion are dangers. Affairs of the houses ruled and tenanted by Jupiter are likely to be important.

Sun to Saturn: A period of seriousness and hard work. The potential for consolidation and learning life's lessons, such as patience and responsibility, is strongest where the more harmonious aspects are concerned, but birth chart reference must also be made. Achievement is possible, in terms of reward for continuing effort and application to duty. Frustrations, difficulties and delays may occur, sometimes illness or loss—check house rulerships.

Sun to Uranus: A period of change, progressive ideas and dynamic activity. Unusual or inventive feelings and occurrences are possible, but it is often a time of highly-strung tension or turbulence —refer to Uranus' chart placing. Unexpected events and erratic behaviour are indicated.

Sun to Neptune: A period of heightened sensitivity. This may be experienced as spirituality, inspiration and refinement, but in the everyday physical world the energies are often distorted and there can be a desire for escape. Confusion and deception may follow, with a feeling of being 'all at sea'. There is a need to experience a degree of letting go (check Neptune's house placing and rulership), but abuse of alcohol and drugs can be a danger.

Sun to Pluto: A powerful period which stimulates personal transformation. All feelings and occurrences are intensified and pushed to extremes, often producing great depths and great heights of experience. Old inner structures may have to be destroyed before the new can be built. Pluto's house placing and rulership may be involved.

Sun and Ascendant: Personal integration. Sun progressing to conjunct Acendant, occurring after the Sun has been in the twelfth house, indicates a period of new beginnings and emergence of individual achievement and creativity. Ascendant progressing to conjunct the Sun suggests a gradual peaking of integration. Other aspects have less strong results, but the more stressful contacts allow integration only with difficulty. Check Sun's house placing.

Sun and Midheaven: A period focusing on externalized affairs. The conjunctions bring the greatest opportunity for worldly achievement, whilst the less harmonious aspects suggest periods of difficulty or testing in matters connected with the externalized environment. Check Sun's house placing.

Mercury—Progressions and Directions
—First refer to Chapter 3, page 47.
—Modify interpretations in respect of sign, house, aspects and rulerships in the birth chart.
—Time period is variable; it may be as short as six to nine months,

but can be several years if a station is involved.

Mercury to Moon: A period of mental changeability. Intuition may be enhanced, but the feelings are likely to affect intellectual objectivity. Instability may lead to difficulties—check natal house placings and rulerships.

Mercury to Mercury: A period of focus on mental activity and communication, with particular reference to house rulerships and placing in the birth chart.

Mercury and Venus: A gentle period, associating with harmony and social interaction. Enjoyable conversation and creative writing are possible, but the less harmonious aspects may present minor difficulties due to frivolous behaviour. Check birth chart placings by house and rulerships.

Mercury and Mars: A period of mental vigour and incisiveness. Increased activity in the local environment is possible and there is opportunity for intellectual progress and for initiative. The more difficult aspects suggest a sharp tongue and impulsive decision making. House placements and rulerships will be especially relevant.

Mercury to Jupiter: A period of mental optimism. Opportunities or success in affairs associated with communication or the mind. Attitudes may be broad in their scope; knowledge may be expanded, particularly in deeper subjects such as philosophy or religion. Difficulties may be experienced through over-optimism or undisciplined thinking—check natal house placings and rulerships.

Mercury to Saturn: A period of mental concentration and serious attitudes. Hard work may be necessary in affairs associated with communication (writing, teaching, learning, etc.) and although this may bring achievement, consolidation and the laying of foundations are more likely. Pessimism, delays and introversion are possible. Refer to house rulerships.

Mercury to Uranus: A period of heightened mental activity and inventiveness. New and unexpected ideas flash and may flow more quickly than they can be handled, but they often enable progress to be made. Nervous tension may be a problem and eccentric or rebellious attitudes can develop. Changes may occur in matters associated with Mercury's placing in the birth chart.

Mercury to Neptune: A period of mental sensitivity and imagination. Communication can be inspired and refined, but the mind may be confused and nebulous, making discrimination difficult. Intuition, dreams and perhaps psychic connections are stimulated, but the person may also be over-impressionable and have judgement impaired. Deception and scandal are possible. Check birth chart placings and rulerships.

Mercury to Pluto: A period of mental depth; transformation of inner attitudes. Desire for research, deciphering life's conundrums and discovering deeper motivations are all possible. The less harmonious aspects correlate with an explosive mentality and the power inherent in the contact may be difficult to handle. Mental instability is a danger, but depth psychology and analysis can channel the energy. The person may become obsessed with collective ideas. Check Mercury's house position and rulerships.

Mercury and Ascendant: A period of mental and communicative activity, particularly associated with the affairs of Mercury's natal house and rulerships.

Mercury and Midheaven: A period of emphasis on extroverted mental and communicative activity in worldly affairs. Associations are likely with the affairs of the houses associated with Mercury in the birth chart.

Mercury Stationary Retrograde: A period of mental introversion, easier to handle later in life than before the first Saturn return; difficult during school years. Check house placing and rulerships.

Mercury Stationary Direct: A period when mental barriers are lifted and communication openings are likely to occur. This phenomenon will always happen within the first twenty-five years of life when Mercury is retrograde at birth. Check house placing and rulerships.

Venus—Progressions and Directions
—First refer to Chapter 3, page 48.
—Modify interpretations in respect of sign, house, aspects and rulerships in the birth chart.
—Likely time period is one to two years, but longer if a station is involved.

Venus to Moon: A gentle and relaxed period of harmony and comfortable reactions. An artistic nature may be stimulated and social contact, particularly with women, is indicated. The less harmonious aspects suggest a somewhat bland indifference and ineffectual self-indulgence.

Venus to Venus: (Only limited aspects possible.) A period of focus on relationships, love, instincts, social affairs and artistic interests. The amount of harmony will depend on the aspect and reference should be made to house placing and rulerships.

Venus and Mars: A period of warm affections or passion. Aspects between these two planets represent contact between feminine and masculine of a more down-to-earth nature than Sun and Moon and can indicate love affairs, marriage and increased sexual activity and enjoyment. Social intercourse is also stimulated. The less harmonious aspects may correlate with problems resulting from impetuous passions. Check house placings and rulerships.

Venus to Jupiter: A period of enjoyment and extroverted affections. Sometimes the two traditional benefics will bring success and abundance, particularly with the conjunction, but the less harmonious aspects stimulate extravagance and indulgence.

Venus to Saturn: A period of control and responsibility in relationships, social contact and artistic pursuits. Marriage is possible under this contact, often to an older or serious person, but any relationships can be stabilized. The more difficult aspects, and sometimes the conjunction, indicate lessons to be learned through difficulty or disappointment in emotional relationships. Self-doubt and underconfidence can occur in affairs connected with Venus, its house placing and its rulerships.

Venus to Uranus: A period of emotional tension and unpredictability. Change or turbulence in relationships and social activity is possible, but unusual and unexpected occurrences can prove exciting and stimulating. Ingenuity and originality may be achieved in creative and artistic matters. Refer to Venus' house placing and rulerships.

Venus to Neptune: A period of sensitivity and rarified harmony. Emotional relationships may become idealized or spiritualized, resulting either in the height of romantic sensitivity or in delusions and deceit. Scandals may occur under the inharmonious aspects.

Artistic inspiration and sensitivity lead to refined creativity or appreciation, particularly appropriate to music and poetry. Check house placings and rulerships.

Venus to Pluto: A period of transformation and inner change in relationships. Compulsiveness and fascination may be experienced and there may be a deepening of any harmonizing activities— artistic interests and socializing, as well as love partnerships. Check house placings and rulerships.

Venus and Ascendant: A period of focus on personal relationships and on the affairs of Venus in the birth chart, its house and its rulerships.

Venus and Midheaven: A period emphasizing relationship, art and beauty in the context of one's position in society. Associations are likely with the affairs of the houses connected with Venus in the birth chart.

Venus Stationary Retrograde: A period of introverting, consolidating or restricting relationships or artistic activities. Check house placing and rulerships.

Venus Stationary Direct: A period of development and opening out in relationships and art, perhaps even a gentle breakthrough. Check house placing and rulerships.

Mars—Progressions and Directions
—First refer to Chapter 3, page 48.
—Modify interpretations in respect of sign, house, aspects and rulerships in the birth chart.
—Likely time period is 1½-2½ years, but can be considerably longer if a station is involved.

Mars to Moon: A period of emotional activity and restlessness. Initiatives may be taken, but quarrels or trouble involving women may occur, possibly due to rash behaviour. Check house placings and rulerships.

Mars to Mars: (Only limited aspects possible.) A period of stimulated energy. Activity, initiative and bold pioneering behaviour are all possible, particularly in affairs associated with Mars' house placing and rulerships.

Mars to Jupiter: A period of enthusiasm and energetic self-expression. With the harmonious aspects it is easier to channel this energy constructively and personal achievement and success may be realized, but over-enthusiasm and recklessness may create a period of destructive activity. Check both planets in the birth chart.

Mars to Saturn: A period of determination and frustration. It may be possible to ground and stabilize one's active energies under the more harmonious aspects, but generally restrictions and difficulties in achieving results are likely. The ability to assert oneself may be thwarted; quarrels and accidents are possible. Frustrations may stir up violent behaviour. Check both planets in the birth chart.

Mars to Uranus: A period of highly charged activity. Assertiveness and maverick behaviour are stimulated. Progress may be made unexpectedly or as a result of unusual or inventive actions. Friction with others and irritability may result from feelings of tenseness Sudden accidents are possible. Check both planets in the birth chart.

Mars to Neptune: A period of rarified energy. The combination of planets is subtly complex and all activity can be inspired and refined, but the less harmonious aspects threaten dissolution and distortion of energy. Desire and passion may be aroused in un-savoury ways and the individual may be prone to undesirable influences. Religious or spiritual zeal is possible. Check both planets in the birth chart.

Mars to Pluto: A period of power and desire. A determined fighting spirit is stimulated and this can achieve much. But ruthlessness and even cruelty are possible if the explosive inner drive takes over and autocratic desires are not resisted. When this potentially violent combination is channelled, great confidence and leadership abilities are stimulated. Both planets rule Scorpio and there will be focus on anything connected with this sign in the birth chart.

Mars and Ascendant: A period of readily available energy. Affairs associated with Mars in the birth chart, its house and rulership will be emphasized.

Mars and Midheaven: A period of activity in career and the external environment. Check Mars, its house and rulerships in the birth chart.

Mars Stationary Retrograde: A period of frustrated energy or introverted activity. Check house placing and rulerships.

Mars Stationary Direct: A period of concentrated and usable energy. Check house placing and rulerships.

The Moon—Progressions and Directions
—First refer to Chapter 3, page 49.
—Modify interpretations in respect of sign, house, aspects and rulerships in the birth chart.
—The time period for aspects of the progressed Moon is around two to three months, and the following interpretive examples concentrate on progressions. Aspects by solar arc direction, moving at the same speed of the Sun, will be active for one to two years and the interpretive comments should be modified accordingly.

Moon to Moon: A phase of heightened emotions. Emotional changes may be experienced, perhaps associated with women or the mother. Affairs of the Moon's house or of the houses associated with Cancer in the birth chart will be important.

Moon to Mercury: A phase of mental activity and fluctuation. Various forms of communication may be stimulated and sensitized; communicative events may be triggered. Affairs of Mercury's house or its house rulerships will be affected.

Moon to Venus: A phase of emphasis on emotional relationships, artistic pursuits or any matters associated with Venus, its house or its house rulerships. Both inner feelings and outer events may be stimulated.

Moon to Mars: A phase of ardent emotions and changeable behaviour. Events associated with Mars, the affairs of its house or the houses it rules may be triggered. Initiative is stimulated; emotional friction is possible.

Moon to Jupiter: A phase of emotional warmth and expansion. A generous nature will be stimulated, but the less harmonious aspects may bring over-extroverted feelings. Affairs of Jupiter's house or rulerships may be brought to the fore.

Moon to Saturn: A phase of serious or disciplined emotions. Restrained or inhibited behaviour is likely. The affairs of Saturn's house or of the houses it rules are emphasized and associated events may be stimulated.

Moon to Uranus: A phase of highly charged feelings. Behaviour may be erratic and unpredictable, particularly emotionally, but attitudes will be inventive and independent. Unexpected events may be triggered off, especially those associated with Uranus and its house connections.

Moon to Neptune: A phase of heightened sensitivity. Imagination, sympathy and idealism are all stimulated, but emotional susceptibility may lead to disappointments. Affairs of Neptune's house or rulership may be highlighted.

Moon to Pluto: A phase of strong feelings and deep emotions. The intensity of this contact can result in extremes of behaviour and radical changes in attitudes and opinions. There is a desire to understand motivations. Pluto's house or rulerships may be involved.

Moon to Ascendant: The conjunction is an important phase when a new personal cycle begins. With all aspects, instinctual and emotional sensitivity is heightened and can allow a tuning-in to the nature of changing opportunities.

Moon to Midheaven: The conjunction is the start of an important new career cycle. All aspects focus on the relationship with the external world and stimulate additional consideration of one's position in society.

Moon through 1st House: The Moon passing over the Ascendant marks the start of a new cycle of individual expression. Focus on personal reactions to all external stimuli from the environment will continue over the period.

Moon through 2nd House: Attitudes to material possessions and to financial affairs are gently emphasized. Emotional reactions, practical values and feelings about one's own self-worth are highlighted and may be reviewed.

Moon through 3rd House: Communications and conversation are more open and responsive. Mental inquisitiveness may be stimulated through reading or interaction with others, but there will also be sensitive reactions, resulting in either better understanding or hurt feelings.

Moon through 4th House: A more passive new cycle starts, reflecting a desire for stability and putting down roots. Feelings of protection and security are stimulated and a period of sensitive introversion is likely.

Moon through 5th House: A period of confidence and responsiveness to creative potential occurs, building from the previous reflective fourth house phase. There is a more extroverted expression of emotions, which will be warm and generous.

Moon through 6th House: A period of emphasis on work activity. There may be a desire to be of practical service to other people. Personal attitudes to health are focused, not only bodily, but also emotionally and spiritually.

Moon through 7th House: An important new cycle involved with close personal relationships begins when the Moon moves over the Descendant. The concept of partnership and one's personal attitudes to it may be re-examined. Social contacts may increase and one's behaviour in relationships is likely to be more emotionally aware.

Moon through 8th House: A deeply feeling period. One often experiences extremes of emotion which may result in personal inner re-evaluations. The more complex aspects of relationships with others—emotions, sexuality, power play and money—are stirred up and seem to need attention. One may become concerned with occult and mystical matters.

Moon through 9th House: A much more actively extroverted phase when one feels the need to search and expand one's horizons. Travel is possible, but a less tangible quest is more likely—seeking knowledge or sharing one's own discoveries with others, perhaps through lecturing or writing.

Moon through 10th House: When the Moon passes over the Mid-heaven a new cycle starts that concerns one's position in the wider environment, probably in society and/or career. Although personal achievement is possible, it is more likely that there is an emphasis on attitudes and feelings towards one's aspirations and material realities in the world—preparation for success rather than its realization.

Moon through 11th House: A period of consolidation of objectives and ideals in life. There is likely to be a greater empathy towards wider humanitarian issues and a more sensitive concern about one's position in society and the contributions made to it. Focus on involvement with friends and groups is possible.

Moon through 12th House: A time of retreat and introspection. Deep inner sensitivity is delicately and subtly tuned into very personal or even mystically spiritual needs. Feelings of solitude may result from letting old methods and supports fall away. It is a time of intimate preparation and building inner strength before the new beginning to come when the Moon reaches the Ascendant.

Mars—Transits
—First refer to Chapter 4, page 54.
—Check Mars in the birth chart by sign, house, aspects and rulerships.
—The transiting aspects of Mars (not detailed here) are effective for only a few days and will have only passing importance. However, they may well act as triggering devices, activators of events relating to other progressions and transits. This is particularly true when these other indicators have an active, energized nature, Mars itself perhaps being involved. The stations of Mars should always be observed and special note made if one falls on (or aspects) a sensitive degree in the birth chart. This phenomenon will be effective for up to about a month. Mars spends six to seven weeks in an average-sized house.

Mars through 1st House: Personal activity and initiative; impulsiveness; energy and single-mindedness.

Mars through 2nd House: Keen focus on money and material affairs; emotionally assertive.

Mars through 3rd House: Activity in local environment; energy directed towards active communication, both spoken and written.

Mars through 4th House: Activity in the home; friction with family members; energetic security seeking.

Mars through 5th House: Emphasis on enjoyment, creative pleasures and extroverted recreation; activity with children, perhaps friction.

Mars through 6th House: Focus on work, a busy few weeks; possible friction with employees or work mates; care needed with health.

Mars through 7th House: Activity in marriage and close personal relationships; quarrels possible.

Mars through 8th House: Deeper emotions and sexuality are stimulated; activity connected with finance and other peoples' possessions.

Mars through 9th House: Desire for travel; activity associated with higher education, philosophy or religion; restlessness.

Mars through 10th House: Focus on position in society; initiatives taken in career; ambitions stimulated.

Mars through 11th House: Energy directed towards impersonal contacts, groups and societies; activity with friends, possible friction.

Mars through 12th House: Activity behind the scenes; possible frustrations and impatience; storing energy.

Jupiter—Transits
—First refer to Chapter 4, page 56.
—Modify interpretations in respect of sign, house, aspects and rulerships in the birth chart.
—Likely time period is around two to three weeks, unless a station is involved. Transits through a house average about a year. The interpretations may be used for directions if time period is extended.

Jupiter to Sun: Extroversion is stimulated and opportunities may occur. An enjoyable time, but the less harmonious aspects may encourage extravagance. Travel is possible and idealistic philosophical attitudes may be felt. Check natal placings and rulerships.

Jupiter to Moon: A time of expanded and extroverted emotions— warmth and happiness, but a tendency to gush. Family affairs may be enjoyed. Check birth chart.

Jupiter to Mercury: A talkative time when ideas are enthusiastically presented. Over-optimism, exaggeration or lack of mental discipline may cause difficulties or exhaustion. Philosophical attitudes stimulated. Check birth chart.

Jupiter to Venus: A time of happiness and ease, with the possibility of a lucky break, but pleasant indulgence is more likely. Favourable for romance. Check natal placings and rulerships.

Jupiter to Mars: A time of increased energy and enthusiasm, but over-exhaustion and excess are dangers. Activity is stimulated and travel may be desired. Check birth chart.

Jupiter to Jupiter: Opportunities are presented in connection with Jupiter's placings and rulerships in the birth chart. Possibility of a new beginning. Optimism is likely, but discipline may be needed to take advantage of the contact.

Jupiter to Saturn: A time of opportunity for hard work and consolidation, but it may be frustrating. Wisdom and judgement may be increased, but lost opportunities are equally possible. Check natal house placings and rulerships.

Jupiter to Uranus: A time of unexpected opportunities and possible lucky breaks. Impulsiveness or exaggerated behaviour is stimulated. Check birth chart placings.

Jupiter to Neptune: A time of idealism and altruism. Religious instinct may be stimulated and intuition is enhanced; unselfish attitudes are experienced. Judgement may be impaired. Check house positions and rulerships, particularly including the strength of Pisces in the birth chart.

Jupiter to Pluto: A time of powerful enthusiasm. Financial affairs and investment may be successful, but gambling is unwise. Increased self-assurance and popularity are possible. Check birth chart.

Jupiter to Ascendant: A new cycle of personal opportunity may start and travel is possible. Optimism and happiness. Check Jupiter's placing and rulerships in the birth chart.

Jupiter to Midheaven: A new cycle of opportunity in career or position in society may be stimulated. Attitudes to achievement are buoyant. Check Jupiter's placing and rulerships in the birth chart.

Jupiter through 1st House: A period of personal opportunity and enthusiasm.

Jupiter through 2nd House: A period of financial buoyancy or material gain is possible, but over-extravagance is a danger.

Jupiter through 3rd House: A period of prolific communication, which could be positive for writers, teachers, lecturers and people in business, but undisciplined idle chatter is also possible.

Jupiter through 4th House: A period of enjoyment in the home and with the family. A new cycle of home life may start, such as a satisfactory change of residence or new feelings of security.

Jupiter through 5th House: A period of pleasurable recreation and perhaps romance or enjoyment with children. Creative activity may be augmented, but reckless speculation should be avoided.

Jupiter through 6th House: A period of enjoying work and obtaining satisfaction in being of service. Possible popularity in the work environment.

Jupiter through 7th House: A period of expansion and optimism in close personal relationships. New beginnings could be either marriage or divorce.

Jupiter through 8th House: A period of deeper expansiveness. More serious enjoyment in relationship is experienced and the sex life may be fulfilling. Financial benefits from others are possible.

Jupiter through 9th House: A period of expanding horizons. Enthusiasm for travel may be increased and new knowledge, philosophies or ideas may be explored.

Jupiter through 10th House: A period of enthusiasm for career ambitions. A successful new worldly cycle may start and opportunities for a better position in society may occur.

Jupiter through 11th House: A period of friendship and wider social contacts. New ideals may be stimulated and enjoyment experienced in group activities.

Jupiter through 12th House: A period of contented introversion. Inner contemplation and self-nourishment is undertaken happily and it is easy to let go of what has outgrown its use. Generosity and unselfishness stimulated.

Saturn—Transits
—First refer to Chapter 4, page 57.
—Modify interpretations in respect of sign, house, aspects and rulerships in the birth chart.
—Likely time period is around three to four months, unless a station is involved. Transits through a house average about 2½ years.
—The interpretations may be used for directions if time period is extended.

Saturn to Sun: A time of personal discipline. The more harmonious aspects may bring constructive hard work and positive extra responsibilities, but other aspects imply harder lessons. Restriction is possible through the affairs of the houses associated with Saturn in the birth chart. A serious attitude or depression may indicate a need to redefine personal objectives.

Saturn to Moon: A time of serious feelings. Emotions can be stabilized, but shyness or even depression may result from inhibition. Illness or difficulty associated with the home or with women is possible. The undesirable effects of old habit patterns may present themselves. Check natal house placings and rulerships.

Saturn to Mercury: A time of mental discipline. Studying and other intellectual work can be successfully carried out under this contact, but the activity may be arduous. Concentration is enhanced, but extroverted conversation is likely to be inhibited. Check natal house placings and rulerships.

Saturn to Venus: A time of consolidation or restriction in relationship. A more serious attitude to partnership may occur because of temporary separation, added responsibility or the need to redefine the relationship. Feelings of underconfidence or inhibition are possible in the affairs of Venus, its house or its rulerships.

Saturn to Mars: A time of disciplined energy. The softer aspects may allow consolidation and practical resolve, but most contacts frustrate and undermine. This may result in feelings of impotence or manifest in harsh or over-assertive behaviour. Accidents are possible. Check the natal placing of Mars and the houses ruled.

Saturn to Jupiter: A time of discipline and patience. Hard work can bring its rewards in time, both materially and in wisdom and maturity, but delays and frustrations may be experienced. Check natal chart placings.

Saturn to Saturn: A time of testing. If awareness and patience are exercised, wisdom can be achieved, for this is when the lessons of Saturn in the birth chart are able to be learned. Re-examine Saturn's position by sign, house, aspect and rulership. (See Chapter 2, page 27.)

Saturn to Uranus: A time of consolidating progressive attitudes. The stabilization of unusual and inventive ideas and behaviour can have very positive results, but the planetary energies are conflicting and stress, stubbornness, rebelliousness or domineering conduct may bring difficulties. The affairs of houses associated with Aquarius are likely to be emphasized.

Saturn to Neptune: A time of practical idealism and spiritual responsibility. The conflicting nature of the planets often brings negative results; over-disciplining the intuition or proneness to deception and trickery may easily cause gross errors of judgement. Check birth chart.

Saturn to Pluto: A time of harsh determination. Ambitions may be realized, but perhaps achieved with a cold ruthlessness. Hardship may result from selfish and unsympathetic behaviour towards others. Check birth chart.

Saturn to Ascendant: A time of personal application. The conjunction represents an important new cycle starting, but all the aspects request hard work and discipline.

Saturn to Midheaven: A time of application in the external environment. Career progress may be consolidated, but hard work and extra responsibility are likely to be required.

Saturn through 1st House: A period of laying foundations. Saturn over the Ascendant is a new beginning, but the consolidation of this requires one to come down to earth and apply oneself to the very roots of the new venture. The period may be demanding, but later rewards reflect the effort put in.

Saturn through 2nd House: A period of material structure. Attitudes to money and possessions are redefined, possibly as a result of financial hardship. Lessons are learned through material affairs.

Saturn through 3rd House: A period of mental discipline. Work at studying and writing is likely. A serious approach to all mental and communicative activity may help to increase confidence in intellectual abilities, but this is unlikely to be achieved without much heart searching.

Saturn through 4th House: A period of serious focus on foundations. Responsibilities of home and family are likely to be demanding. Serious considerations or redefining of attitudes may be made in terms of one's personal base and security as a new fourth house cycle starts.

Saturn through 5th House: A period of determined self-expression. This serious look at having fun can result in creative energy being applied with great discipline. The person may feel insecure and unlovable, making demands on others in consequence. There may be extra responsibilities associated with children.

Saturn through 6th House: A period of attention to work. Discipline in any work carried out can result in greater efficiency, but taking on too much and overworking may create health problems. Discrimination must be learned.

Saturn through 7th House: A period of responsibility in partnerships. Lessons must be learned through one's close relationships with others. This may involve marriage responsibilities or difficulties—or consolidating or redefining one's attitudes to the relationship with spouse or lover.

Saturn through 8th House: A period of inner examinations. A serious and disciplined attitude is taken towards the deeper aspects of relationships with others and transformation may occur after some difficulty. Extroverted emotions may be inhibited and sexual confidence may be impaired. Financial lessons are learned and there may be contact with the occult. Experience is gained from involvement with the use or abuse of power.

Saturn through 9th House: A period of consolidation of knowledge and of self-improvement. Formal further education or a disciplined programme of individual study and reading may be started. One is likely to take a serious look at basic life beliefs and these may be redefined. Hard work may be associated with travel.

Saturn through 10th House: A period of focus on life ambitions. A new career phase is likely to start, often associated with frustrations and increased responsibilities. Sometimes success and recognition occurs, but more usually there is a need to re-evaluate and define one's position in society and the wider environment.

Saturn through 11th House: A period of defining duty within the community. Whereas the tenth-house transit focused on personal achievement, this defines impersonal responsibilities and one's wider purpose in life within the collective. Altruism and social conscience may be stimulated.

Saturn through 12th Houe: A period of inner review and analysis.

This is a time of lonely self-examination, when one must learn to release the old structures and outmoded methods of behaviour in preparation for the new building period to follow when Saturn reaches the Ascendant. The dissolution of old values may be bewildering, but the ability to look deep within allows new seeds to be planted and to germinate.

Uranus—Transits
—First refer to Chapter 4, page 61.
—Modify interpretations in respect of sign, house, aspects and rulerships in the chart.
—Likely time period is around one to two months unless a station is involved.
—Interpretations can be modified for directions by extending the time period.

Uranus to Sun: A time of unexpected change. Inventive, progressive or rebellious feelings may be stimulated and changes may possibly occur due to new personal contacts. Positive results are often likely, but erratic or perverse behaviour may cause disruption of a non-constructive nature. Check the house position and rulership of Uranus in the birth chart.

Uranus to Moon: A time of highly charged emotions. Changes associated with the Moon's house or rulership are possible and feelings and reactions may be unpredictable. Intuitive originality and experimentation are likely under the more harmonious aspects; unsettling changes and emotional tension are possible under other aspects.

Uranus to Mercury: A time of mental originality and inventiveness. Sudden flashes of brilliance are possible, but mental restlessness or eccentricity may cause difficulties. Changes may occur in the affairs of the two planets' houses or their rulerships.

Uranus to Venus: A time of heightened feelings in relationships and harmonizing instincts. There is a need for originality and perhaps experimentation in partnership and artistic matters. Under the less harmonious aspects break-up of relationship is possible. Check placings and rulerships in the birth chart.

Uranus to Mars: A time of restless, but assertive energy. There is a desire for independence, which may turn to rebellious defiance, but a resourceful magnetism can achieve much. Turbulence and change associated with the relevant houses and rulerships may cause difficulties. Accidents are possible.

Uranus to Jupiter: A time of stimulated originality and opportunity. Unexpected new ideas are possible, often associated with more profound subjects. Tense over-enthusiasm and reckless behaviour may lead to mishaps. The affairs of the relevant houses and rulerships are important.

Uranus to Saturn: A time of change to structures. This may be stressful if the established order resists change, but a constructive attitude and inventive practicality are equally possible. Stubbornness and defiance may cause difficulties. Check birth chart placings.

Uranus to Uranus *: A time of re-evaluation and change. Positive break-throughs can be achieved under all aspects, but stress and tension are possible—particularly if the transitions are resisted. (See Chapter 2, page 30.)

Uranus to Neptune *: A time of inspired illumination. A higher level of consciousness may be achieved, but there are possibilities of weird obsessions and mental instability. Check natal houses and rulerships.

Uranus to Pluto *: A time of inner awakening. There may be a powerful urge for reform and a strong inner purpose, but there are dangers from destructive tendencies (inner or outer) and explosive crises may result. Check birth chart placings.

Uranus to Ascendant: A time of personal change. This may be unexpected upheaval, but it is generally a necessary throwing-off of outworn methods and old situations. Uranus' house placing and house ruled are likely to indicate areas of change.

Uranus to Midheaven: A time of externalized change. Position in society or career is likely to be affected, but the opposite angle is also affected and home life may also be subject to disruption or evolution. Check natal position of Uranus.

Neptune—Transits
—First refer to Chapter 4, page 63.
—Modify interpretations in respect of sign, house, aspects and rulerships in the birth chart.

—Likely time period is around two to three months unless a station is involved.

—Interpretation can be modified for directions by extending the time period.

Neptune to Sun: A time of heightened receptivity to intangible energies. Spiritual sensitivity and higher aspiration may help intuitive activities, but the less harmonious aspects bring confusion, impressionability, poor judgement and escapism. Check placings in the birth chart.

Neptune to Moon: A time of finely tuned emotional sensitivity. Compassion and sympathy are increased, but there is proneness to illusion. Dreaminess and emotional disappointments may result. Psychic qualities can be stimulated. Check both planets in the birth chart.

Neptune to Mercury: A time of increased imaginativeness. Mental sensitivity is stimulated, which may bring inspiration and possibly psychic experiences. If too much fantasy fills the mind, muddled thinking and deception (of oneself or by others) can result. The affairs of Mercury's natal house and houses ruled may be affected.

Neptune to Venus: A time of heightened sensitivity to all forms of harmony. Artistic capabilities, especially musical, may be uplifted and an almost spiritual attitude to relationships may develop. But excessive romanticism and idealism can bring disappointments, difficulties or even scandal. Check birth chart placings.

Neptune to Mars: A time of subtly influenced energies. Action may be inspired by some ideal, but distortions are likely in the form of deceit, injudiciousness and an unwillingness or inability to make necessary effort in given circumstances. Check Mars' house position and rulerships.

Neptune to Jupiter: A time of high ideals and generosity. There may be an increased interest in spiritual matters and an optimistic attitude for the future. Affairs associated with Pisces in the birth chart will be highlighted, but poor judgement and unrealistic ideals may bring problems.

Neptune to Saturn: A time of inspired realism. Ideals and religious attitudes can be channelled in a constructive manner; inspiration and imagination may be used practically. Under the less harmonious aspects there may be frustration, suffering, insecurity and imprudent action. Check natal house placings and rulerships.

Neptune to Uranus *: A time of uplifted far-sightedness. Higher imagination and inventiveness may be taken to a new level of inspiration, but there are dangers of becoming entangled in illusions and unreality. Check placings and rulerships in the birth chart.

Neptune to Neptune *: A time of contact with intangibility. This can be inspiring and may bring spiritual sensitivity, but illusion, deception and fog are also possible results. Check Neptune's natal house and rulership.

Neptune to Pluto *: A time of inspired transformation. There may be unusual descent into the depths or a transcending of limitations. However, these extremes can also result in total impracticability or a plunge into degeneration. Check birth chart placings.

Neptune to Ascendant: A time of heightened personal sensitivity. This may bring a feeling of being out of touch with reality, resulting either in positive idealism, spirituality and musical or artistic inspiration or in confusion, daydreaming, failure and escape. Check natal house and rulership.

Neptune to Midheaven: A time of worldly inspiration. Altruistic ideals may be strengthened and public image may be affected, beneficially or otherwise. Hidden trickery and manipulation may occur in career or position in society. Check natal house and rulership.

Pluto—Transits
—First refer to Chapter 4, page 65.
—Modify interpretations in respect of sign, house, aspects and rulerships in the birth chart.
—Likely time period is around two to four months unless a station is involved.
—Interpretations can be modified for directions by extending the time period.

Pluto to Sun: A time of symbolic death and rebirth. An inner power struggle results in deep changes that are not easy to handle unless the need for transformation is accepted. Contact with collective energies may bring out a desire for external power. Check natal house placings and rulerships.

Pluto to Moon: A time of emotional intensity. Feelings are given great depth and power, but may appear to be one-sided. Explosive reactions are possible. Affairs connected with the Moon's house and house ruled (and Pluto's) are likely to be affected.

Pluto to Mercury: A time of investigation and inner searching. There is a desire to uncover meanings and motivations and to carry out research. Mental attitudes may be transformed—personal psychological work can allow this to happen constructively, but mental disturbances and obsessions may occur. Check natal chart placings.

Pluto to Venus: A time of deep changes in harmonizing instincts. The need for relationship and one's involvement in it are stimulated powerfully and compulsively, but under the less harmonious aspects upheaval or break-up can occur. Creative abilities may be intensified. Check birth chart.

Pluto to Mars: A time of powerful desires. Ambition and drive are stimulated and energy levels augmented, but harshness and ruthlessness may also be present. Base desires and insensitivity may cause ill-considered actions resulting in difficulties. Check house placings and rulerships in the birth chart, especially affairs associated with Scorpio.

Pluto to Jupiter: A time of resourceful enthusiasm. Feelings of penetrating truth-seeking are likely; confidence is instilled. Problems may occur as a result of impulsive behaviour and possibly fanaticism. The affairs of the two planets' houses and their rulerships are likely to be involved.

Pluto to Saturn: A time of powerful persistence. There will be a focus on purpose and ambitions, which may be worked towards by austere self-denial or a harsh selfishness. However, privation and hardship may be imposed from external sources. Check natal house placings and rulerships.

*Pluto to Uranus**: A time of deep changes. These may not be outwardly apparent, but can manifest as desire for independence and the creation of new frameworks. Various crises may occur. Check house placings and rulerships in the birth chart.

*Pluto to Neptune **: A time of transcendence. There is a deepening of ideals and the opportunity for consolidation of spirituality, but distortion can occur and problems may arise from fanaticism and spiritual confusion. Check birth chart placings.

Pluto to Pluto *: A time of focus on inner change. The meaning of Pluto in the birth chart and the affairs of its house and the house it rules will be emphasized.

Pluto to Ascendant: A time of personal transformation. There are likely to be changes of a deep and significant nature and new personal resources may be revealed, often after some discomfort. The affairs of Pluto's house or house ruled may be involved.

Pluto to Midheaven: A time of transformation in externalized affairs. Radical change in one's position in the world is indicated, probably career affairs or possibly home life. This may involve a need for recognition. The affairs of Pluto's house or house ruled may be involved.

*Note on Outer Planet Transits

The transits of the three outer planets to their natal positions very often have a non-personal effect. Because so many individuals were born with these planets around a certain degree, such slow transits will be affecting a large number of people at the same time. This does not mean that there will be no effect for the individual, but some people will be more sensitive to the transits than others. It depends on levels of consciousness and inner evolution, but where one of the outer planets is strong in the birth chart (e.g. angular, prominently aspected or chart ruler) the transit will be felt more strongly.

7.
SOLAR AND LUNAR RETURNS

'Many happy returns' is a phrase in such common use that we hardly think what it means when we wish someone, in effect, 'Happy birthday!—may you have many more.' But it certainly reflects the concept of the solar return, for this is the moment when the Sun reaches the exact degree of the zodiac that it held at birth. This occurs once every year around the birthday, but not necessarily exactly on the day itself. The chart that is set up shows the planetary positions, Ascendant and houses for this moment and is known as the solar return chart. It indicates the nature and pattern of the following twelve month period. The Ascendant and ruling planet are especially significant and prominent houses indicate a focus of activity and events. However, the solar return chart must always be read in conjunction with the birth chart—indeed it can be regarded as a snapshot of the transit positions for the true birthday each year. Cross reference between planets, houses and, to a lesser extent, signs in the birth chart and in the solar return chart is an essential exercise for interpretation.

It is generally accepted that the solar return chart refers to the whole twelve month period, although some astrologers believe that the chart is like a struck gong whose strength of sound gradually diminishes. The latter opinion is not supported when one considers that the timing of events during the year suggested on the solar return chart can often be shown by progressions and transits in the birth chart or even by those in the solar return chart itself. Other timing indicators are the lunar returns.

The Moon takes just over twenty-seven days to move through all the zodiac signs and so it returns to its natal position slightly more frequently than once each month—thirteen times each year. The charts set up for these precise moments are the lunar return charts and each represents for the period of a lunar month what the solar return represents for a year. This is how the thirteen lunar returns can also help to indicate the timing of events suggested in the solar return.

Because the degrees of the Ascendant and the house cusps are especially important in solar and lunar return charts, accurate calculation is essential. Movement of one minute of arc in the Sun's position represents about twenty-four minutes of time which corresponds to six degrees movement on the Midheaven. If the birth time is not known accurately, the Sun's position may be wrong by a minute or two of arc and the angles in the solar return chart will be correspondingly inaccurate. Where the birth time is more definite, or when the chart has been reliably rectified, the Sun's position must be calculated to the nearest second of arc so that an accurate solar return chart can be drawn up.

How to Calculate the Solar Return

Example: Prince Charles 1980

1. Take the birth position of the Sun in degrees, minutes and seconds.   22° 25′ 19″

2. Find the nearest Sun position in the ephemeris around the birth day (noon or midnight depending on your ephemeris).   Noon 14 November 1980   22° 16′ 44″

3. Find the Sun's daily motion in 24 hours (subtract earlier day from later).   15 November   23° 17′ 11″ —
                  14 November   22° 16′ 44″
                              1° 0′ 27″

4. Find the difference between the Sun's birth position and noon or midnight (subtract 2 from 1 above).   22° 25′ 19″
                                   22° 16′ 44″
                                  00° 08′ 35″

5. Express this movement in the Sun's position as an amount of time (see below for alternative methods).   If 1° 0′ 27″ = 24 hours therefore:
00° 08′ 35″ =
3 hours 24½ minutes

6. Calculate the chart in the normal way using the time interval found. Acceleration on interval should be used. The birth latitude and longitude is preferred although there is some controversy as to whether the place of residence is more relevant. Some astrologers even maintain that the place where the individual is on the actual birthday should be used.

Time Interval is
3 hours 24½ minutes
after noon.

Alternative Methods of Finding the Interval

a. *Arithmetic*

This method may be laborious, but is infallibly accurate.

$$\frac{0°\ 08'\ 35''}{1°\ 00'\ 27''} = \frac{Interval}{24\ hours}$$

$$\frac{8.583\ minutes}{60.45\ minutes} = \frac{Interval}{24\ hours}$$

$$\frac{24 \times 8.583}{60.45} = Interval$$

$$3.4076 = 3\ hours\ 24.456\ minutes$$

b. *Logarithms*

The tables in the back of *Raphael's Ephemeris* are given only to four places of decimals and are not accurate enough for the solar return calculations. This example uses the *American Book of Tables*, which includes logarithms to five places of decimals.

Subtract Interval log from 24 hour motion log and convert this log result into hours and minutes.

$$
\begin{aligned}
1°\ 00'\ 27'' &= 2.22471\ log \\
0°\ 08'\ 35'' &= 1.37697\ log\ - \\
\hline
result\ \ \ \ \ \ \ \ &\quad 0.84774\ log
\end{aligned}
$$

which converts to 3 hours 24½ minutes

c. *Proportional Tables*

This is the simplest and quickest method. Find the column in the proportion tables headed 1° 0′ 27″ for the 24 hour motion of the Sun. Within that column, find 0° 08′ 35″ and read off the hours and minutes at the side. In the *American Book of Tables*:

$$0°\ 07'\ 33'' = \ \ 3\ hours$$
$$0°\ 01'\ 00'' = 24\ minutes$$

Interpreting the Solar Return

As with everything in astrology, the solar return chart represents potential—in this case the potential pattern of the twelve-month period ahead. The chart is subsidiary to the birth chart and should be seen as representing possible expression over the year of what is shown in the birth chart. Remember that the solar return positions are the transits on the birthday and that that chart is almost an inception chart for your personal year, perhaps even an annual horary chart.

Thus the first interpretation step is to observe where important birth chart planets fall in the solar return chart. The birth meaning of these planets—character, potential, strengths, weaknesses and lessons to be learned—will express during the coming year in affairs relating to the house placements and affected by aspects to those planets and by sign placing. This applies to all planets, but the Sun will by definition always be in the same sign and Mercury and Venus can only ever be in one of three and five signs respectively. These observations will show the ease or difficulty with which the natal chart indicators may express.

The next step is to consider the solar return chart independently. The most sensitive indicator is always the Ascendant, followed by the other angles. The solar return Ascendant shows the personal expression for the year, modifying but in no way obliterating the natal Ascendant. The Descendant sign shows the tone or style of close personal relationships; the MC is the extroverted expression in the wider environment, especially career; the IC shows the somewhat more introverted disposition in relation to basic foundations and security, especially home and family.

The position of the chart ruler, by house, sign and aspect, shows the main focus of personal expression as represented by the Ascendant and whether it will be effected with ease or difficulty during the year. The house placing of the Sun and aspects to it will also point to a major focus for the year's activity. Similarly, the house, sign and aspects to the Moon are important, but these will indicate response and reactions to circumstances and will suggest the temperament of emotions and feelings. Any stellium or grouping of three or more planets will also emphasize that particular house, especially if Sun, Moon or ruler is present, and may increase the importance of the sign in question—but this is less important, particularly since one of the most commonly occurring stelliums involves Sun, Mercury and Venus; in the solar return chart the Sun sign is fixed. Angular planets will have a particularly strong influence, bringing the quality and energy expression of the planet to affairs associated with the angle conjuncted. Other interpretative considerations will also be relevant—aspects to angles, house rulers within the chart, etc.—but the major points are the ones given above.

Next comes the detailed and multifarious possibilities for cross-referencing between the natal chart and the solar return chart. These are best listed as follows:

(a) Each natal planet has a house, aspect and sign placing and rules one or more natal houses. That planet's solar return placing will show where and how in life during the year those birth chart activities (represented by the natal houses involved) and those natal characteristics (represented by aspects and sign placings in the birth chart) will express.

(b) The ruler of the solar return chart has a house placing in the natal chart. The affairs of that natal house will be highlighted in some way during the coming year—they will be brought to the surface and will demand attention. Interpretation of the solar return chart in general and the ruler in particular will suggest the way in which this will happen.

Rulers of the other angles and houses in the solar return chart can be treated similarly but with subsidiary importance.

(c) The solar return Ascendant rules or connects with a natal house and the rising sign may connect with an additional house. The affairs of any house thus indicated will also be brought to the fore during the year. If the solar return rising sign is the same as the natal rising sign, a year of important integrative potential is suggested.

(d) If an aspect contact between two planets in the natal chart is repeated in the solar return chart, the interpretation of that natal aspect will be emphasized during the year, modified by the solar return interpretation. For example a natal Sun square Mars, which can be difficult to handle, may find easier more constructive expression during the year when the solar return has Sun sextile Mars.

(e) Look for mutual aspects between planets in the solar return chart and the natal chart. These indicate links between the meaning of the one planet in the birth chart and the expression of the other in the solar return chart. For example, solar return Moon conjunct natal Saturn suggests sensitivity, reaction and feeling connected with the lessons of natal Saturn. Solar return Saturn conjunct natal Moon points to an emotionally restricted or disciplined year. Solar return Venus conjunct natal descendant indicates the likelihood of an important relationship or blossoming of existing relationship.

However, these mutual aspects must be read with a sense of proportion. They are also transits of the natal chart which occurred on the birthday and Moon transiting conjunct Saturn, for example, would have been within orbs for only a few hours. Mutual aspects are not to be given high interpretative priority.

Timing of Events

The most reliable timing indicators are found in the transits, progressions and directions of the natal chart covered elsewhere in this book, but extra information can be gleaned from the solar return chart. Transits by the faster-moving planets over sensitive points in the solar return chart can sometimes provide indications. Attention should be given to transits of the Sun (and sometimes the Moon) over the angles and important planets—the Sun symbolizes the hour hand of a 365-day clock. As already mentioned, the lunar return can provide a timing indicator of the same genus as the solar return. It is calculated and interpreted in a similar manner but refers only to a lunar month. Thus if the solar return indicates a dramatic change of career during the year—Uranus conjunct Midheaven, for example, then one lunar return out of the thirteen for the year which also shows a particular emphasis on career (e.g. stellium in tenth house) or a prominent Uranus (conjunct Midheaven or Ascendant, close aspect to the Sun, ruler or Midheaven ruler for example), then that is likely to be the month when the career change suggested in the solar return will be constellated.

Few astrologers have time to work professionally with lunar returns, nor are there many clients who are prepared to pay for this amount of work. However, home computers are becoming much more available to astrologers and are within financial reach of more people. Thus it is hoped that the use of lunar returns as well as solar returns will become a viable forecasting tool for an increasing number of people.

Interpretation examples are given in Chapter 9.

8.
OTHER TECHNIQUES

Converse Progressions

The rationale behind secondary progressions, that each day after birth equates with each year of life, can be extended in various ways. One of these variations is to make each day *before* birth also equate with a year of life. This system is known as converse secondary progressions and the positions are calculated in the same way as for normal progressions, but the noon or midnight date will be different and must be calculated in *reverse*.

Many people find the idea of converse progressions unacceptable, but if one accepts the day for a year rationale of normal progressions, it is only a widening of that acceptance to allow the principle of converse application. Converse progressions (sometimes referred to as recessional progressions) have been of particular interest to theosophists and other people for whom the philosophical implications of reincarnation are important. They state that, whereas the days after birth, the normal progressions, provide opportunities for us to exercise our free will and modify our karma, the converse progressions are inextricably involved with our past and therefore refer to our past karma or the circumstances of this incarnation, which are with us because of occurrences and choices made in previous incarnations. This may be true, but it seems to be applying a one-sided logic to the matter. For any given birth chart, both the converse and the normal progressions are equally certain in the timing of their aspects, which is when the individual has to react to them, and the mere two or three months before or after birth seem only tenuously linked with the differentiation between past lives and future potential in this life. A helpful analogy may be to consider a pebble dropped into a pond. The pebble can be seen both as an event and as the moving aspects correlating with it; the ripples spread out in all directions.

Directions (as opposed to progressions) may help the sceptic to accept the converse concept, for if the Sun by normal direction reaches Venus, then by definition Venus by converse direction will conjunct the Sun. The converse concept can be applied to tertiary and minor progressions (described below) and also even to transits. The latter are cumbersome to work out and few astrologers have time to go into this degree of detail or sophistication in regular work, but I do recommend at least trying the converse transits and the converse progressions in one or two personal charts that are well known.

It is worth noting that the cycles in converse transits will unfold at very similar rates to normal transits. A person's normal Saturn return, for example, will occur at much the same time as their converse Saturn return, but the converse transits over other planets may occur at any time. In a chart where Pluto has made no major aspect to the Sun, for example, converse transiting Pluto maybe a surprisingly revealing indicator.

Tertiary and Minor Progressions

The day for a year rationale can also be extended in other directions, almost without limit. If the basic premise is accepted, then that day in the ephemeris can be taken to correlate with not only a year of life, but also with a month or a week. If it is equated to a day of life, sudenly a new rationale or description of our friend the logical, dependable old transit is discovered! The ephemeris might even be taken to equate with an hour, minute or second of life, but the planetary tables needed to work with this would be vast in their extent and the resulting movements, much faster than conventional transits, would be of little practical use.

Equating a day with a month produces an interesting rate of movement of the planets, faster than secondary progressions, but slower than most transits; counting twelve days in the ephemeris for each year (i.e. twelve months) of life is a simple, if laborious process. But the question immediately arises that a calendar month, variable in its length, is a somewhat arbitary, man-made time limit. The astronomical precision of the lunar month should be preferred, even though it makes the counting of the days in the ephemeris much more difficult. There are tables available to facilitate this in *Progressions*, by Chester Kemp and, for the calendar month method, in *The Technique of Prediction*, by R. C.

Davison (see Bibliography). One day for a lunar month is the method for tertiary progressions; the obscure correlation with a calendar month is known as 'monthly secondaries'.

A further variation is known as minor progressions, where a month in the ephemeris equates with a year of life. This rate of motion is faster than tertiary progressions, but still slower than transits. C. C. Zain and the Church of Light School of Astrology developed minor progressions. Both these monthly-based progressions result in workable movements of planets which might otherwise be less relevant; for example, Pluto and Neptune move too slowly to have any effect by secondary progressions and transits of the personal planets are too fast to be worth interpreting. Tertiary and minor progressions allow for additional trends from these planets.

Primary Directions
All progressions and directions discussed so far are based on the relationship between the Earth and the Sun. Primary directions are based on the daily rotation of the Earth on its axis: the time taken for one degree of right ascension to move across the Meridian (roughly four minutes of sidereal time) equates to a year of life. There are two major disadvantages in this system. First, the calculations are formidably complicated and laborious, involving trigonometrical formulae. Second, accuracy of birth time is essential and each four minutes error gives one year inaccuracy in forecasting; this is similar to the reliability problems of the secondary progressed Ascendant and Midheaven. For mathematical enthusiasts, there are books that describe the calculation techniques, but for the non-trigonometrical primary experimenting enthusiast some computer services do offer calculation of primary directions.

Daily Progressed Angles
Hidden in the approximate one degree movement annually of the progressed Midheaven and Ascendant is the fact that each makes one complete circuit of the zodiac in addition to that extra one degree. Thus, during any year the daily progressed angles will move through all the signs and houses at a rate of just under one degree per day. The days when the angles reach natal planets are said to have particular importance in the nature of the contact involved; intermediate house cusps can also be used. This is another system which depends on an accurate birth time if it is to be remotely relevant and reliable.

The Daily Chart

This is a system, written about by Sepharial, where a chart is set up for any given day using the original time of birth. Thus it can be viewed as a sort of daily solar return; if the birth latitude is used, rather than the place of current residence, the Sun will be in the same house as at birth. It should be a useful device for those individuals who are reluctant to leave home each day without seeking permission from the planets.

The Graphic Ephemeris

It is said that many scientific people who are sceptical of astrology have been convinced of its validity when confronted with a graphic ephemeris. The statement sounds a little far-fetched, but certainly the visual presentation of the ephemeris for the year, showing the movement of the planets as curving lines across the page, gives a clarity not found in the planetary tables and might well make a sceptic at least take a second look at astrology.

The graphic ephemeris was developed by the German school of Rheinhold Ebertin and his son Baldur and therefore it relates to the 90° dial system of that school. It enables one to see transiting contacts at a glance—but only the conjunctions, squares, oppositions and 45° aspects. These are admittedly the more consequential aspects, but anyone who uses semi-squares and sesqui-quadrates would be foolish to omit the quincunx, which I regard as a stronger aspect; the graphic ephemeris does not show it. Nor does it show sextiles and trines—and it is pleasing to observe the more harmonious contacts, even if their effect is gentle and though they are easily smothered by the harder aspects. The graphic ephemeris (Prince Charles: 1981) is illustrated in Figure 5 and it will be seen that the elapse of the year is expressed on the horizontal axis and the degrees of the signs on the vertical axis. 45° aspects (half of the 90° dial) are shown on the right hand side and, on the left, three separate columns indicate the cardinal, fixed and mutable sign groupings and their degrees.

Natal planets are inserted by drawing a horizontal line for each at the degree of the sign for the appropriate column. The outer planets' transiting movements for the year are relatively flat undulating lines, while the fast-moving planets are seen as nearly vertical lines. The Moon is not marked, but full and new Moons and eclipses are shown with a circle on the Sun's line. Thus, where any transit line cuts one of the horizontal natal planet lines there is

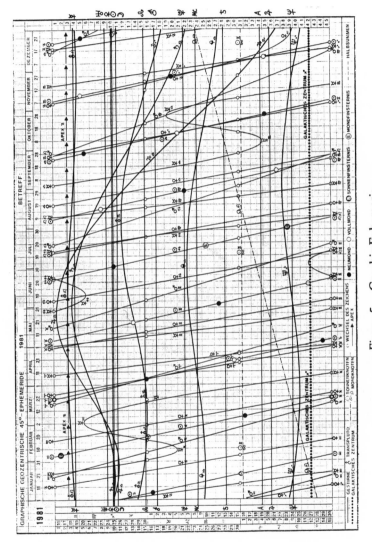

Figure 5. Graphic Ephemeris.

either a conjunction, square, opposition, semi-square or sesqui-quadrate taking place. Natal aspects of this nature will show as the horizontal lines being near each other, but since an 8° orb represents nearly one-fifth of the vertical scale, the natal aspects are not obvious unless nearly exact.

The graphic ephemeris gives a broad overview of the year and is particularly useful for spotting a build up of transiting activity concentrated in a few days—there will be many lines intersecting on the graph. Such a concentration, especially when the faster-moving planets are involved, is not always easy to see in the conventional ephemeris. The shortcomings of this presentation are the lack of certain aspects showing at all and the fact that natal planets at the top and bottom of the graph may be missed when considering certain transits.

Rectification

All astrologers like to work with an accurate chart, but most birth times are not recorded accurately. One of the uses of precise forecasting techniques is to work backwards with events in life that have already happened and, by trial and error, find the most likely Ascendant and Midheaven for the chart. The exercise is imprecise and the word rectification implies a greater degree of accuracy than is usually achieved. It is a complex and lengthy process and, having completed it, the weary astrologer may feel that his ego deserves the reward of having achieved 'rectification' in the dictionary sense of 'correction; exchanging for what is right'. But the word also means 'amend and adjust', and I prefer these less dogmatic implications.

The most reliable method of rectification is as follows. First, make as detailed as possible a list of all the major events in the life of the person whose Ascendant is uncertain. Second, starting with the most important events, work out all the astrological significators for that time and see how they apply to that event. If the Ascendant and Midheaven are known approximately, draw a rough chart showing the possible ranges of the angles. If the time is unknown, observe what events do not appear to have adequate astrological indicators and see if there are any contacts to apparently blank parts of the chart—one of the angles could be there. Always use the progressed Moon and the inclusion of directions and tertiary or even minor progressions is recommended; converse movements can also be useful. In rectification, masses of detail will often reinforce and confirm, unlike forecasting where it will more likely confuse. It is easier to fit astrological influences to past events than to put a finger precisely on the future occurrence that will fit the astrological influences. Strangely enough, although they must be used, transits may be less helpful. This is because there is often a wider sphere of influence from the collective nature of a transit—as observed earlier in this book, progressions have a more personal relevance.

Many astrologers try to avoid the demands of proper rectification by judging what house position is most appropriate for the Sun, by placing a certain planet angular or by correlating an Ascendant to the physical appearance. Sometimes they may be right, but one should see these methods only as well-informed guesswork. They are not reliable and, although they may help to narrow down six possible rising signs to four, they cannot dependably be substituted for correlating aspects with past events.

A final supposed method of rectification is the pre-natal epoch. This epoch, or period of time before birth, is said to show the moment of conception. Thus if you know when the child was conceived, hey presto! you know the exact moment of birth. That reasoning is suspect in itself. The epoch calculation is complex and needs the birth time to be known within half an hour. Zip Dobyns, in her useful book on rectification, outlines (with little enthusiasm) the steps to be taken for this calculation. The chart for the moment of conception would be very useful to work with for that individual *if we could be sure of its accuracy*, but I am extremely dubious of the whole method. Any grain of validity is crushed if the birth was artificially induced, but I have not been able to verify the pre-natal epoch theory even in cases of natural births. Some people claim symbolic validity for the epoch chart, but even they will admit that it probably does not represent the actual physical moment of conception and many discount its use in rectification. The most damning objection to its use in rectification is to observe that identical twins, presumably, have the same pre-natal epoch, but are nevertheless born at different times.

Astrological Birth Control

This seems a not inappropriate point to examine the possibilities of birth control through astrology. A Czechoslovakian psychiatrist, Dr Eugen Jonas, claimed that, in addition to the normal ovulation cycle, women have another fertility cycle based on the angle of the Sun and the Moon. When the Lights are at the same angular relationship in the sky as they were at birth ($\pm 15°$), the woman is at her maximum fertility, but outside this range the woman will not conceive. However it is necessary to check the normal ovulation cycle in relation to this astrological cycle. Dr Jonas also maintained that the sex of the child was determined by whether the Moon was in a male or female sign at the time of conception.

Many women, disliking artificial forms of birth control but prepared to accept conception if it occurred, have tried this method of birth control with apparent success, but it must be emphasized that the medical and statistical evidence is certainly inconclusive, if not discouraging. Dr Jonas' work in Czechoslovakia, until it was banned by the Communist authorities, concentrated more on helping apparently infertile women to conceive and a greater success than the conventional medical profession was claimed—in what is the reverse of birth control. Moon sign at conception indicating the sex of the child is also unproven statistically, but the fact that sperm can live within the woman's genital tract for at least five days makes it effectively impossible to be sure of the Moon's sign at the moment of conception. Finally, one of the rules of pre-natal epoch theory states that the Moon's position at conception gives either the Ascendant or Descendant at birth. From Dr Jonas' theory, all men would therefore have masculine signs rising and all women would have feminine signs—obviously not true. Of the two, I prefer to disbelieve the pre-natal epoch theory—but of course they may both be wrong. (For those interested in further reading on this subject the best book available in English is *Astrological Birth Control* by S. Ostrander and L. Schroeder; Prentice Hall, New Jersey, 1972. The paperback is by Bantam books, titled *Natural Birth Control*.)

Harmonic Directions

This system of forecasting (strictly speaking not a 'direction') is very new and is quite unlike any of the other methods discussed in this book. It was proposed around 1975 by John Addey, the great British astrologer and philosopher, as a logical extension of his thinking on the harmonic basis of astrology and it is included in the Diploma course of the Faculty of Astrological Studies. The theory is that all astrological effects (signs, houses, aspects, decanates, degree areas, etc.) can be best understood in terms of two factors— number and cycle. Thus, all astrological meaning is seen to derive ultimately from the divisions by number of particular circles or cycles; for example, the diurnal cycle presents the houses, the month correlates with the lunation cycle and the year gives the zodiac.

This concept can be seen most clearly in the case of aspects. The opposition, for example, results from the division of a synodic cycle by two, the trine by three, and so on. By studying in a Pythagorean manner the ideas and archetypal processes that are expressed by numbers, we can come to an understanding of the meanings of the aspect or division in question. In this way it is possible to examine divisions by any number.

Addey went on to suggest that we can study the workings of any particular number process in the psyche by making the whole birth chart 'vibrate' to the number in question. To do this we simply multiply the position of each chart factor by the number concerned and create a new harmonic chart with the multiplied positions that result. The new Ascendant is placed in its usual position on the East side of the chart, but the Midheaven may fall anywhere.

If we want to study the workings of 'two-ness' and polarity within the psyche, we multiply the basic chart positions by two. The simplest way to do this is to set down the chart positions in absolute longitude (degrees and minutes from 0° Aries), and multiply this position by the number under consideration. If the result is more than 360°, then substract 360° a sufficient number of times to reduce the answer to less than 360° For example: Sun 16° 20′ Taurus = 46° 20′. In the second harmonic chart, the Sun will be at 46° 20′ × 2 = 92° 40′ = 2° 40′ Cancer. Moon 15° 10′ Scorpio = 225° 10′, which × 2 = 450° 20′. This is greater than 360°. Subtracting 360° gives 90° 20′ = 0° 20′ Cancer. Thus, the natal Sun Moon opposition with an orb of 1° 10′ becomes a conjunction with an orb of 2° 20′ in the second harmonic chart. All chart positions are calculated in the same way and placed on a new chart. In practice, it is simplest to use either a calculator or harmonic chart tables—and most chart computing services now supply these calculations.

Harmonic charts can be of great value in sophisticated character analysis, but Addey went on to suggest that, at any particular year in our life, we will vibrate or resonate to the number of our age. Thus at age twenty-five, we have circled the Sun twenty-five times since birth. This will put us in sympathy with our own 25th harmonic chart and our life will give expression to the patterns of energy which it contains.

Harmonic charts will change dramatically from one year to the next, like chords and harmonies in a piece of music. They usually seem to present a vivid image of the year as a whole and should be used for indications of the main themes in the life; they can be interpreted similarly to solar returns. Unless the birth time is very accurately recorded the angles should not be relied on since, for example, an error of one degree would produce an error of 32° by age 32. This very factor, however, enables harmonic charts to be used as an additional tool in rectification. In practice, each harmonic chart seems to start its relevance some three weeks or so before the birthday. Prince Charles' 32nd harmonic chart is shown on page 147 (Figure 14).

Historical Note: Unknown to Addey, the Swiss astrologer, K. Hitschler, hit upon a similar method of directing in the late 1940s, but it was unconnected with the concept of harmonics. He suggested that a body's distance from 0° Aries was its natural arc of direction for any year.

9.
FORECASTING IN ACTION

In this chapter various examples are given to illustrate the different forecasting techniques covered in this book, with the exception of the less common methods mentioned in Chapter 8. I have chosen to use the charts of HRH Prince Charles and HRH Diana, Princess of Wales, not only because of their topical interest at the time of writing and the arrival of their first child, but also because of their lasting appeal, both in the UK and world wide. Comparison of their charts (synastry) is covered in another book in this series.* No example chart is ever ideal (a fact which serves as a reminder that every chart is entirely idiosyncratic). Charts of public figures and members of the royal family have the disadvantage that collective influences and demands beyond the simple working out of personal destiny can distort the individual and personal correlations with the astrological influences. But I feel sure that these charts will be of wider interest than John Robinson and Eileen Smith, hypothetical unknowns from my case files.

The natal charts of Princess Diana and Prince Charles, showing progressions and transits for 1981, are given on page 123 (Figure 6) and page 132 (Figure 9) respectively. A detailed examination of the period before and after the wedding, 1980-1982, is given for Princess Diana, and examples of broad trends are shown for Prince Charles. Each of their solar returns for the year covering the wedding is illustrated and discussed and Princess Diana's lunar return is shown for July 1981. Prince Charles' harmonic chart for the year of his marriage is shown and discussed briefly.

*Penny Thornton, *Synastry: A Comprehensive Guide to the Astrology of Relationships* (Aquarian Press, 1982).

Princess Diana

The detailed information for Princess Diana is listed on page 124 (Figure 7) and an example of the Faculty of Astrological Studies progressions worksheet is shown for her for 1981 on page 128 (Figure 8). In 1979 Lady Diana, as she then was, soon to be eighteen, was feeling the effects of progressed Sun opposite Saturn. For any young woman towards the end of her formal education, this progression would bring a serious attitude to life, perhaps making her wonder what difficulties might lie ahead and what responsibilities the adult world would bring. Neptune started transiting her Ascendant in 1978 and was a major influence through most of 1979, so it is likely that there was a degree of confusion and lack of direction contributing to her serious Saturnian attitude. Natal Neptune is in the tenth house and rules the third, suggesting that her uncertain thoughts concerned what she might do with her life (career) and possibly matters associated with communication and education—either questions about her own further education or working in the Pimlico infant school. Neptune squares the ruler Jupiter in the birth chart, giving idealistic and romantic tendencies, so it is possible that her thoughts were also turning towards whom she might marry: perhaps she was even then falling in love with her prince—but the Saturn progression might have made such thoughts seem hopeless in reality.

A number of very different influences were increasing in strength as 1980 came in. The possibly depressing effects of Saturn were diminishing and being replaced by the background influences of progressed Ascendant opposite Mercury; Jupiter directed by solar arc to opposite Uranus and Neptune was transiting in aspect to Venus, Uranus, Moon and Midheaven. Natal Mercury is both in the seventh house and rules it, so it has a direct bearing on close personal relationship. Neptune now influencing Venus, the planet of relationship, and the Moon, not only Sun ruler but a co-ruler of her seventh house, suggests heightened emotional sensitivity and real romance. The stage was set not only for relationship to blossom, but also for change—Uranus is involved as well. Any Jupiter/Uranus contact has the potential for sudden unexpected opening out and for surprise opportunity, and this is emphasized here because Jupiter is the ruler of the chart. Further change was also guaranteed by the opposition of Uranus to Venus—traditionally to do with relationship, but also, in Diana's chart, connected in some way with career and position in society; Venus rules the Midheaven. Uranus was within orbs of this opposition from January through to April 1980 and then again in October, neatly showing us now that unexpected change can be beneficially exciting and not necessarily destructive, as this aspect is sometimes rigidly interpreted. Uranus was also squaring the Moon and natal Uranus, triggering off that important emotionally charged T-square in the birth chart. We should also observe the occurrence of the first quarter of the Uranus cycle a little earlier than the theoretical twenty-one years.

Another important cyclic indicator occurred around April when the progressed Moon reached the Midheaven, heralding the start of a new 28-year period connected with that very position in the world

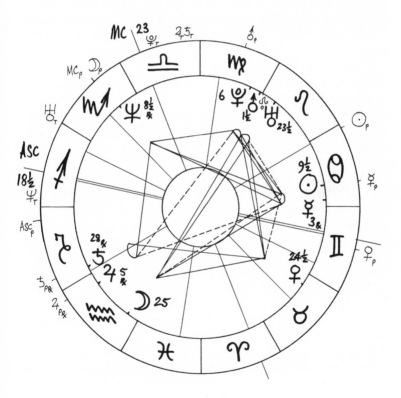

Figure 6.   Princess Diana's Birth Chart. 1 July 1961; Sandringham, 7.45 p.m. Progressions and Transits for 1981.

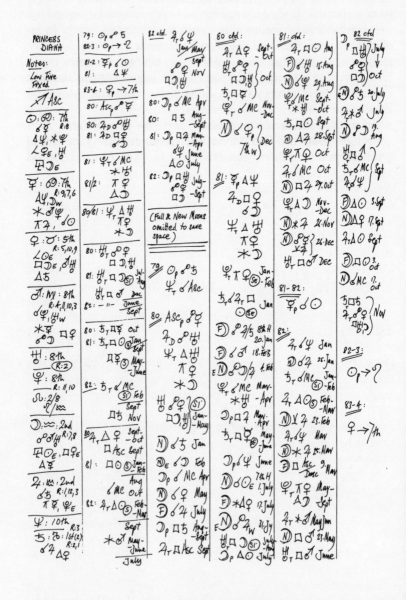

Figure 7. Princess Diana's Data.

which may have been a source of preoccupied concern only a year before. A series of New Moons kept the early months of the year busy with feelings of new beginnings—responsibilities, emotions, relationship—as conjunctions with Saturn (January), Moon (February eclipse) and Venus (May) took place. It can be seen that many of the moving indicators were picking up her critical 23°-25°, plus Saturn at nearly 28°. Where any chart has an above average number of planets on similar degrees of whatever signs they are in, there is always a strong resonance throughout the chart when moving indicators touch these degrees—in any sign.

In July 1980 the Full Moon was conjunct ruler Jupiter and emphasized the second to eighth house axis—own possessions and other people's; own feelings and self-worth and other people's emotions. Through the autumn, Saturn and Jupiter applied discipline and joy in varying measure, an astrological influence to follow even more noticeably in the following year as the young woman moved from her ordinary if privileged life to the pressures and happiness, the responsibilities and reward of being married to the heir to the nation's throne. Jupiter moved in trine to Venus and squared the Ascendant, but the progressed Moon squared Saturn and transiting Saturn squared Mercury. The joy of literally finding her prince and yet the secrecy and the red tape of protocol were mixed in a frustrating pressure. But whatever decisions beyond her control were being made at this time, astrologically the time of complete and radical change was inexorably drawing nearer. We may observe the new Moon falling three degrees from her seventh house cusp (one is tempted to speculate whether she was born a little earlier, but that is the unacceptable face of rectification and other factors do not confirm it!) and, for what it is worth, also falling close to her progressed Venus. But the decisive planetary factor was Pluto transiting onto her Midheaven for the first of three contacts —November-December 1980, March-April 1981 and September-October 1981, representing a year of transformation with regard to her position in the world.

This major transit was certainly the dominating influence during 1981, the year of the wedding. Pluto also started to aspect Venus and the Moon (the sextile with Uranus is more or less submerged beneath the other activity, but it gives a strong background of inner change and outer change coupled positively) and this continued into 1982. In January and February 1981, Pluto was stationary in exact quincunx to Venus, 'transforming relationship', and again

emphasizing the Midheaven which Venus rules. Venus also rules
the fifth house in which it is placed and the transit indeed pointed to
a love affair of deep and significant portent. Directed Jupiter also
moved on to contact Venus and the Moon—last year's happy
surprises now confirmed as love and relationship. Neptune
continues to sensitize the T-square planets, bringing romance,
glamour and idealism—the princess-to-be was floating on air. However, the other aspects did not allow anything like a total escape into
this fairytale come true.

The year started with an exact stationary square of both transiting Saturn and Jupiter to the natal Sun. It is particularly interesting
to see the way in which this transiting conjunction resonated with
the same (but wider) conjunction in the birth chart only weeks
before the announcement of the engagement on 24 February. It is
conjunct the second house cusp natally, a paradox affecting
material possessions and personal feelings, and no doubt in January
1981 came the true realization of what it was going to be like to be
instantly the most sought-after news item in the world and to have
the burden of this lack of privacy for the rest of her life; and yet also
to be about to be officially engaged to Great Britain's most eligible
bachelor and to be in love. Natal Saturn is in Capricorn, and the
lessons of material achievement, structure and aspirations—both
sought and feared—would also have been touched by the transit at
this time.

Full and new Moons reverberated through the year. January saw
a full Moon on the cuspal second to eighth axis again, conjunct the
mid-point of the Jupiter/Saturn conjunction. In February the solar
eclipse fell on the Moon/Jupiter mid-point and the full Moon
opposed Mars. Emotion reached peaks of feeling in the build-up to
the wedding as progressed Moon squared Jupiter in the spring and
conjoined Neptune in June. But the demands of protocol, privacy,
bodyguards and restraint of freedom were ever present, concentrated astrologically in Saturn squaring Mercury, stationary and
exact, during May and June.

Uranus made three squares to the seventh house co-ruler, the
Moon—a station in early 1980 starting the change; a transit in
November, perhaps when serious consideration was being given to
the possibility of announcing the engagement; then a final station,
one degree off exact, a week after the wedding. The new Moon
before the wedding was an astrological classic—exact to within ten
minutes of arc conjunct natal Sun in the seventh house: she was

married within the month. The following full Moon, twelve days before the wedding, was in exact sextile to Venus and the solar eclipse two days after was within three degrees of the opposition to Jupiter. Progressed Moon trined Sun during this period and Jupiter squared Sun in August. The August lunations conjuncted Uranus and Pluto, planets which had each been active by transit for a much longer period—it was a firm underlining of an astrological signature. Saturn was present in the post-wedding period, reminding the Princess of the duties and responsibilities she had taken on—it squared the Sun in September. But the expansive optimism of Jupiter was persistently emphasized all through the period. The transiting conjunction with the Midheaven—tritely, 'success and opportunities in the world'—was almost literally eclipsed by a series of new Moons aspecting natal Jupiter from September 1981 through to March 1982. It is unusual to experience such a sequence, but delightful that the new beginnings should be proclaimed with such optimism. Trine-September; square-October; sextile-November; semi-sextile-December; eclipse conjunct-January; semi-sextile-February; sextile-March, all within one degree of exact aspect.

At the time of writing, early in 1982, the aspects for this year show increasing responsibility and some change—hardly surprising for a young woman who has just become the wife of the heir to the throne and is expected to give birth to a future King or Queen around her own birthday. Let us examine just some of the many indicators. The major progression affecting the current period from autumn 1981 through 1982, peaking in early summer, is progressed Mercury conjunct Sun. As a slight digression, it is worth noting that her retrograde natal Mercury went direct in 1969, around age eight, when her parents divorced. Progressed Mars was conjunct Pluto and Uranus squared the Sun during the following two years, so we can assume that the dissolution of the marriage was an explosive period followed by change for the young Diana, but a time when she was able to come out of herself in some way. Perhaps her parents' honest statement about the irretrievable nature of their marriage was a catharsis which, although unsettling, had positive results. Returning to Mercury in 1982, the conjunction with the Sun focuses on mental confidence and communication, but above all on union in her marriage—both these planets are in the seventh house; one rules the seventh, the other the eighth.

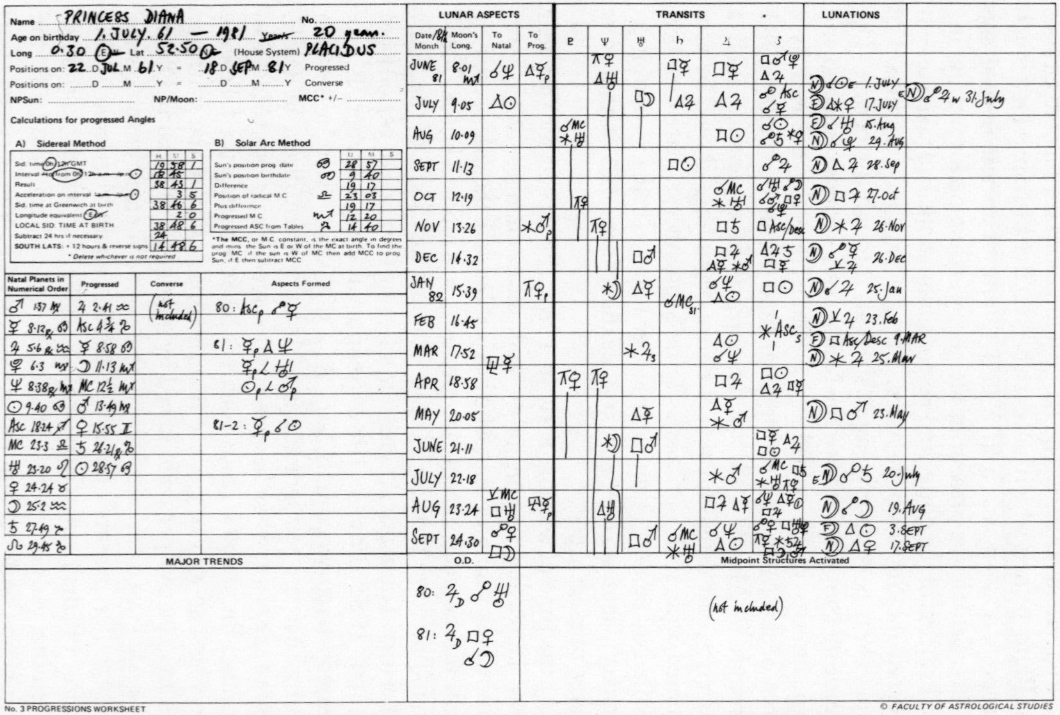

Figure 8. Princess Diana's Data (Faculty of Astrological Studies form).

After Jupiter's promises and benevolence comes the duty and hard work brought by Saturn transiting in 1982 over the Midheaven in January and February and later in September. Saturn also squares its natal position once in November, a gentle rehearsal for her Saturn return in 1990. Change is shown in the background by the completion of Pluto's quincunx to Venus and trine to the Moon and in the foreground by Uranus squaring Mars—December 1981, June and September 1982. Progressed Moon squares Uranus and contacts the important $23°$-$25°$ during the summer. Mars rules the fourth house and so one level of interpretation is to talk of moving house and having the decorators in, but it also refers to the Princess's roots and psychological base in life—those, too, are changing. It activates the Mars/Uranus conjunction in the birth chart as well, that rebellious temper and ability to flare up unpredictably; she will wish she could smash the press reporter's camera over his head and she has already put her foot down and demanded to take her baby on official tours with her.

Uranus is likely to be exactly squaring Mars at the time of the birth and Pluto aspecting Venus and, less closely, the other planets and angles on those degrees. These are not especially tranquil contacts, which could point to a difficult birth; but Venus both in and ruling the house of children in its own sign of Taurus in the natal chart should help to counteract this. It may well be that it will be the Princess who will be difficult with the elite and very proper royal medics involved with the little heir's arrival.

Whether she gives the midwife a hard time or not, the Princess has positive progressions developing in the future. Late in 1982 the Sun moves into Leo, helping her at an appropriate time to assume the regal mantle, confident, proud and benevolent. In 1983 another lunar cycle begins as the progressed Moon passes over the Ascendant and, soon after, progressed Venus moves into the seventh house. This will emphasize her marriage and she will no doubt consolidate it with more children (fifth house), but Venus also rules the tenth house and it is likely that the emphasis on the marriage will be reflected in greater involvement, as a couple, in public affairs. 1985 shows change in her life as Uranus transits over her Ascendant and Pluto squares ruler Jupiter. This coincides with Prince Charles' progressed Sun's reaching natal Jupiter and opposing Uranus—new opportunities and change. Since Saturn transits over his Sun this year too, many astrologers have speculated that he will have added responsibility within the royal family, perhaps even taking over the monarchy. The Queen's Sun is opposed by Pluto in 1984 and 1985 and she also reaches her second Saturn return, so such conjecture is astrologically well founded. But a full evaluation of these possibilities requires mutual analysis of all the relevant charts, including the various Great Britain charts themselves, and that leads us too far from the intention of this book, nor is there space to encompass it. Perhaps you, the reader, are by now so well versed and enthusiastic about the subject of astrological forecasting that you will feel encouraged to examine these charts yourself!

Prince Charles

All public figures have two lives—one that the rest of the world sees and another personal life. With some famous people one feels that the public image, the glamorous persona, becomes all-dominant and that the real human being within has atrophied; with others the inner man may sometimes be glimpsed. In the case of Prince Charles it is different—the real person is very much alive, but is also fused with the public figure, the monarch to be. From birth, and perhaps before, the first child of the then reigning king's daughter had destiny thrust upon him and a moulding and grooming process started which would not only assist him in the life of national responsibility that inescapably lay ahead, but also perhaps enable him to sustain and survive it.

When we examine the moving trends in his chart (see page 132, Figure 9) over the years, we must remember that the pure and simple expressions of the astrological influences are always modified by the external demands of his position. The reactions of the inner man himself may be obscured—certainly most of them will be kept confidential by the requirements of protocol. But this does not prevent us interpreting the indicators and also looking at some of them as if they applied to an ordinary man. This will help to illustrate the ranges of possibilities which exist in all astrological forecasting work.

The broad trends in Prince Charles' life are shown on page 133 (Figure 10) and I have selected certain years for comment where his life was particularly active or where the astrological indicators are more interesting. The Uranus transits early in his life were not particularly significant, mainly because there were no other major progressions or transits in effect (unlike the Uranus conjunction with the Sun in 1980, the year before his wedding); but there are nevertheless interesting correlations. In 1956 and 1957 Uranus passed over the Ascendant three times and it was in January 1957 that the young prince first went to school, initially as a day boy and later in the year as a boarder at preparatory school. Although these events would be entirely natural for an upper class eight-year old, the transit suggests quite an upheaval. It was also just after the first square of Saturn to its natal position. Prince Charles was the first heir to the throne ever to actually go to school (private tuition was more normal) and for the small boy it must indeed have been a bewildering experience. He had obviously led a sheltered life; he had never been anonymously in a crowd, had never gone shopping and had not handled money—that strange stuff with his mother's picture all over it. Indeed he is reported to have asked the Queen around that time: 'Mummy, what are school boys?' During his first year at Cheam Preparatory School, Saturn made three transits over Mars, ruler of his tenth house and co-ruler of his Sun. This is not a comfortable transit, being an imposition of restriction on the Sagittarian, independent and free-ranging Mars energy in his birth chart and it is likely that the first year away from the royal household, living among young commoners, was a testing period—part of the monarch-moulding which was inevitably to be his experience. Prince Charles remembers the first few days at Cheam as the most miserable of his life and the following summer as an occasion of 'acute embarrassment', when he was created Prince of Wales and cheered not only by Welshmen at the Commonwealth Games in Cardiff, but also by his schoolmates. Uranus also transited square his Sun in 1960 and 1961 during his time at Cheam, before he left in 1962 to go to Gordonstoun, and this suggests astrologically that the experience of his first school was more of an upheaval for the boy than the much more extrovertedly tough experiences of the Scottish public school. Progressed Sun was square Saturn during 1961 also. However, Uranus moved on to conjunct Saturn, shattering structures, during his first year at Gordonstoun and it was around this time that progressed Ascendant reached Pluto. It should be noted that his brother, Prince Andrew, was born in early 1960, but there is little biographical evidence to suggest that this event caused further change in his life.

In October 1967 Prince Charles went to University—Trinity College, Cambridge. By this time Uranus had moved on and was less influential, although the first quarter cycle, square its natal position, occurred three times—twice stationary (st. January

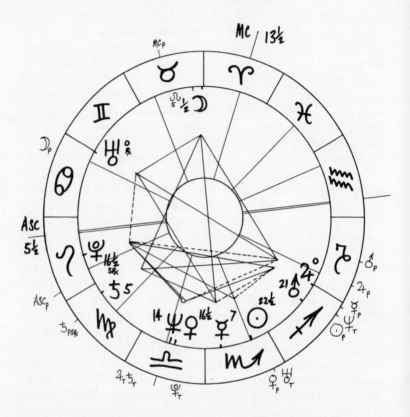

Figure 9. Prince Charles' Birth Chart. 14 November 1948; London,
9.14 p.m. Progressions and Transits for 1981.

1968, September 1968 and st. June 1969). Progressed Mars was
trine Saturn and influence from both Pluto and Neptune was increasing; Pluto was sextile Sun on and off from late 1967 through
to the summer of 1969, the first stimulation by transit of his powerful Scorpio-emphasizing Sun square Pluto at birth. Neptune moved
over the Sun through 1967 and in 1968, not only bringing the uncertainties and bewilderment of being the first heir to the throne to
genuinely experience living with his subjects, but no doubt also
bringing an intangible sense of inspired purpose into his life, a realization, for example, that he could receive help from the nation's
prayers and be nourished by them. As transiting Neptune moved
on, progressed Sun applied to the sextile of natal Neptune,

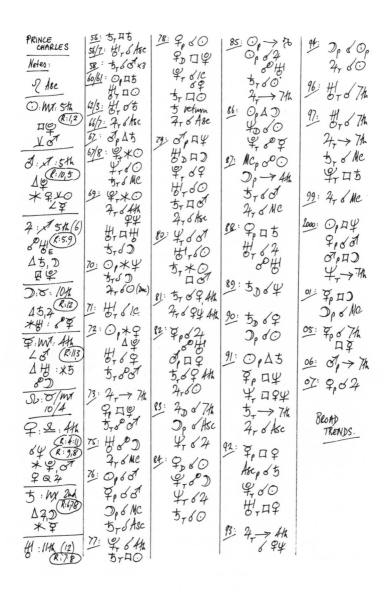

Figure 10.   Prince Charles' Data.

emphasizing this mysterious planet's qualities throughout the three-year period at university. A young man of ordinary birth might well have responded to these influences by dropping out a little, perhaps even 'spacing out' with escapist experimentation with drugs. This would of course be unthinkable for Prince Charles, but one biography does state that 'he was beginning to take an interest in wine' at this time! There are also suggestions that the idealist in him was touched and he evidently pondered on radical politics and even attended one student demonstration, incognito. However, his fellow undergraduates could never really be at ease with him and it was a lonely period, perhaps emphasized by Saturn transiting over the Midheaven in 1968 and over the Moon in 1969 and 1970, remaining in his tenth house throughout his time at university.

Neptune also contributed to his interest in amateur dramatics and he thoroughly enjoyed taking part in the Cambridge revue. But this planet also heightens sensitivity, and with the comfortably transformative Pluto sextile Sun (Pluto rules his fifth house of fun, relaxation and love affairs—also the house where his Sun is) and the transit of Jupiter over his Venus/Neptune/I.C. conjunction (late 1969) it was during his time at Cambridge that he discovered the opposite sex. It was something of a revelation to observe well-educated, liberated girls behaving unlike his well brought up conception of what 'nice girls' do—there were many entirely nice girls living active sex lives with great enjoyment. Prince Charles' first love was Lucia Santa Cruz, the Chilean Ambassador's daughter, three years older than him, worldly wise and beautiful. There have been suggestions that the late Lord 'Rab' Butler, then Master of Trinity, gave constructive support to this affair to 'help Prince Charles enjoy the dwindling days of as private a life as he would ever know'. Lucia, now married to a Chilean lawyer (her first child has a royal godfather), was followed by Sibella Dorman as the prince's lady friend and she apparently once had to climb back into Newnham College after a late night date with the prince.

The Investiture of the Prince of Wales occurred on 1 July 1969 at Caernarvon, coincidentally the eighth birthday of his wife to be. As a ceremony it was a magnificent state ritual not to be matched until his coronation sometime in the future, but an angry minority of Welsh nationalists used the occasion to publicize their cause with ructions and some bombings. Astrologically, Uranus had been stationary just a few weeks before, square to the exact Jupiter/Uranus opposition in Prince Charles' birth chart, simply interpreted as unexpected favourable occurrences and influences, but it is not without the tension of the natal opposition exact to within two minutes of arc. Pluto was almost exactly sextile the Sun on the day and Venus was separating from the opposition to the Sun. Saturn was stimulating the natal Mercury Saturn sextile by transit, involving sixth house (work and service) and eleventh house (objectives, ideals and humanitarian enterprise) by rulership.

During the years after university Prince Charles took on more royal engagements and moved into a position of greater responsibility within the royal family. He trained in the Royal Air Force and the Royal Navy, gaining his wings as a qualified pilot and also learning to fly helicopters. In the royal tradition he spent most time in the Royal Navy and took command of a mine hunter in 1976, which was his last year in the services. However, it was during this time that his various love affairs became a subject of continuous interest in the world's press and speculation about who would be the future Princess of Wales was always present. Prince Charles has a Scorpio sexuality and, with Mars and Jupiter in Sagittarius, has something of a roving eye; the fifth house of love and romance is also emphasized. So it is not surprising that the world's most eligible bachelor had his pick of beautiful women the world over and no doubt enjoyed that old naval custom of having a girl in every port. 'Kissing the prince' became an unofficial ritual by female admirers at some point on every tour, enjoyed by dusky negro samba dancers, Indian filmstars and bikini-clad Australian girls alike. The list of girls in his life at this time stretched from Princess Marie-Astrid of Luxembourg, to actresses Susan George and Farrah Fawcett-Majors and to President Nixon's daughter. Assault by the press was inevitable and the prince learned to relax and (almost) enjoy it; at least he kept his sense of humour. Once on safari in Kenya he presented one news hound with a home-made stuffed bird, complete with blonde wig, asking mischievously if this was the mystery blonde bird the press had been looking for.

Throughout this period there were many astrological indicators suggesting romantic activity. 1972 was his first year as a Lieutenant at sea and this coincided with progressed Sun sextile Venus and Uranus transiting over Venus—romance and changing affections. Because of the exact natal Venus sextile Pluto, progressed Sun was also trine Pluto at this time, reminding us of the deeper, transformative element of that year. Progressed Venus squared Pluto in 1973 and Jupiter moved three times over the seventh (relationship) house cusp and perhaps this emphasized the emotional importance of Lady Jane Wellesley in Prince Charles' life. She was the bookies' favourite in the royal marriage stakes in 1973 and 1974, but she was too independent and liberal-minded to want the life of a future queen—and perhaps to be 'acceptable'. In 1978, at the time of his Saturn return, Prince Charles may well have had one of his more important romances—certainly this must have been when he began to seriously consider choosing his wife. Progressed Venus was conjunct the Sun, a classic relationship indicator, but deeply turbulent Pluto was also active, transiting Venus and the fourth house cusp and being squared by Venus by solar arc direction. Both Susan George and Princess Marie-Astrid were in evidence at this time, but neither could conceivably have become his wife—one an actress with a past love-life and the other a Roman Catholic. Astrologically, he could have been deeply in love with either woman (that could almost have been safely *predicted* for a commoner), but perhaps the demands of his position did not allow him such emotional indulgence. Saturn, ruler of both his relationship house and the sixth house of work and service, first squared his Sun (September 1977 and stationary to one degree in April 1978) and then returned to its natal degree, the Saturn return, in September 1978—ever-present reminder of duty and responsibility. This was his astrological coming of age and, coupled with such an additional build-up of astrological indicators, whatever serious affections he may have felt for any girl he could not marry, or however much he enjoyed his bachelorhood, it must have been the time when he realized that his destiny and duty called.

Prince Charles' wedding was not, in itself, the major change in his life that one might have expected. The two years before show much more strongly that it was the *decision* to marry, settle down (in so far as his life allows it) and give up the pleasures of life as a sought-after bachelor, that represented the greater change. Later in 1979, and twice during 1980, Uranus conjoined the Sun (August 1980 stationary one degree from exact) and Saturn imposed its demands by squaring Mars, sextiling the Sun and, in 1981 and 1982, transiting over the fourth cusp and his Venus/Neptune conjunction. This could be interpreted either as a restriction in relationship or a stabilization. Observing the happiness and euphoria surrounding the wedding, one is inclined to feel that his marriage represents positive and happy stability—and this is borne out by the transit of Jupiter into the fourth house and over Venus and

Neptune just after the wedding. Indeed, for Prince Charles, it is as though the changes and responsibilities will be taking a little time to sink in and become accepted, for it is in 1983 and 1984, following Jupiter's transit over the Sun, that the marriage really blossoms. Neptune uplifts and romanticizes as it transits Jupiter and, by solar arc direction, Jupiter enters the seventh house and Venus reaches the Sun. The progressed Moon starts a new cycle as it comes to the Ascendant and the opposition of Pluto to the natal Moon may transform and deepen his emotional feelings in a very private and personal way—the Moon rules the twelfth house. But this opposition formed by the transiting Sun ruler emphasizes the fourth to tenth axis and Pluto's call for symbolic death and rebirth may signal the arrival of royal destiny. This is echoed by the first contact of Saturn conjunct the Sun in December 1984.

The indicators for 1985 point to an unquestionably important year—even his taking over the monarchy, unlikely though it seems at the time of writing. If he were not a prince, how would we view the progressions and transits at such a point in his career? Progressed Sun conjunct Jupiter—opportunity, success, expansion and perhaps a pinnacle of fulfilment; progressed Sun opposite Uranus—a period of unexpected change and upheaval, progressive influences and untraditional occurrences. Progressed Sun also moves into Capricorn, changing the overlay influence on the natal Scorpio from free and easy Sagittarius to dutiful, aspirational and executive Capricorn—it is over the few years when the change of sign actually takes place that the effect is most noticeable. In the summer of 1985 Saturn transits stationary conjunct the Sun emphasizing duty, responsibility and restriction. Legitimate interpretation would suggest a change of work, bringing success, possibly travel (Jupiter rules ninth), but heavy extra responsibility or hard work, all of which may involve the marriage (Uranus rules seventh). The following years provide few extra clues—progressed Sun trines Moon, progressed Midheaven opposes Sun, Jupiter transits the Midheaven and the progressed Moon starts a new fourth house cycle. 1988 is more interesting: progressed Venus squares Saturn and the Uranus half-cycle is reached. For an ordinary person one might suspect marriage troubles, but for an heir to the throne the changes could be more to do with tenth and eleventh house matters (Venus rulership) and sixth house service. Is it too far-fetched to see coronation as a symbolic marriage of a king to his nation-wife?

Princess Diana's chart is not without activity over these years, reflecting her husband's, as might be expected. Uranus transits the Ascendant in 1985—unexpected changes for her, followed by progressed Ascendant opposite Sun and by Pluto square Jupiter, her ruler, in 1986. A new Saturn Ascendant cycle starts in 1987 and progressed Sun opposes Jupiter in 1988. If the Princess was to become a queen around this time, the pressures of such responsibility would be great because she would not have completed the first Saturn cycle. Pressures, whatever her royal status, are shown astrologically first by Saturn and then Uranus opposite the Sun and then the confusion of progressed Sun square Neptune at the time of the Saturn return in 1991. This is followed by the inner upheaval of Pluto opposite Venus in 1992 and 1993. The former year is another significant one for Prince Charles, when the progressed Ascendant reaches Saturn, Pluto transits the Sun, resonating with the natal square, and Uranus transits Venus. For an ordinary couple, turbulence in the marriage aggravated by broader life changes could be forecast, but since the transformative energy of Pluto is involved in both charts and since we are dealing with the charts certainly of future monarchs, if not by that time of an actual king and queen, then a less parochial interpretation must be considered. The national charts should be examined and those of the other major world powers; the charts of other key people in the country, statesmen and politicians, should also be included in such a study. Where major astrological activity occurs in a prince's or a king's chart its reverberation spreads much wider than the domestic scene. Although 1992 does not look like a particularly easy year for the royal couple, it is almost impossible for domestic or personal difficulty to be detached from the affairs of state. Indeed, it is more likely for the latter to be the major cause of any personal pressures. The years up to the change of the millennium are quite possibly going to be critical in the very history of planet Earth itself and countries and their rulers may be affected in a more individual sense than single people themselves, who will be merely parts of the collective. But those people are still the subjects of their monarchs, where they are fortunate enough to live in countries that still have royalty, and they are in a position to give their good will, support and prayers to the members of the royal family who are their symbolic leaders. Cynical progressivists may criticize the monarchy, but the British heritage of kings and queens is a long and sturdy line, archetypal in quality and providing a unique nourishment to the psyche of the country and its people. May we all support it in every way we can, through whatever changes the future may bring.

Prince Charles—Solar Return 1980/1981

In many ways the solar return for Prince Charles, covering his wedding, is an astrological classic, with the Sun/Uranus conjunction in the seventh house, and it provides some good examples of the interpretive methods used. The chart is shown in Figure 11.

The emphasis of the chart is on the sixth and seventh houses— service and marriage. The natal fifth house Sun moves from its fun-loving, romancing position to the seventh house of marriage. The natal ruler of the seventh house, Uranus, moves from the eleventh

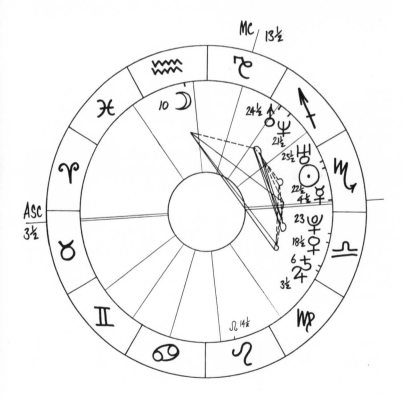

Figure 11.   Prince Charles: Solar Return Chart, 14 November 1980.

house to the seventh in the solar return chart, while the co-ruler Saturn moves from second to sixth. The fourth house Venus/Neptune conjunction splits to sixth house and eighth house respectively, but they remain in aspect, this time a co-operative sextile. Indeed, Venus, ruler of the chart and planet of relationship, retains contact with all its natally aspected planets (except the minor quintile to Jupiter) and all these solar return aspects are harmonious. This suggests that the sensitivity, lovingness and romance, expressing particularly in affairs of home and family, as seen in the birth chart, in the 1980/1981 year under examination, are applying particularly in the deeper emotional side of relationship and in work and service.

The Taurus Ascendant implies stability, sensuality and possessive feelings—and natally it falls in the tenth house close to the Moon, emphasizing career responsibilities, a fact reflected by the Capricorn Midheaven in the return chart. One might have expected to see planets in the tenth house of this chart, but the broad impression given is much more of a year of relationship combined with sixth house work and service, not fame, fortune and publicity. We should remember that the chart is Prince Charles' and does not necessarily reflect how he was seen by a populace struck by engagement and wedding fever. The Moon in the eleventh house (and in Aquarius like Princess Diana's) points to more distant goals, to objectives and ideals, and it is interesting to see that his natal grand trine is retained with trines from the Moon to the Jupiter/Saturn conjunction in the return chart.

Sun in the seventh house is conjunct Uranus, indicating both change and marriage. The important natal Sun square Pluto is retained in the return chart by a gentle, but exact, semi-sextile, which allows comfortable transformation during the year. Moon is opposite Mercury natally in the tenth and fourth houses and this aspect is picked up by a square in the return chart with Mercury angular. There are few so-called difficult aspects in the chart, but Mercury is one planet with both a square and semi-square. One might speculate that Prince Charles and his fiancée had their moments of verbal disagreement during the months before the engagement and the wedding, perhaps more than might be expected. Certainly communication is emphasized—perhaps even some extra discussion with his mother, the Queen, because of the aspect to the Moon; a close semi-square to Mars, one of the seventh house rulers, also suggests some heated reactions. The Jupiter/

Saturn conjunction is placed as well as can be expected, with only a semi-square from the Sun to Saturn marring the picture—Saturn reminds one of duty through its sixth house placing and tenth house rulership. Generally, a lot of the inter-planetary contacts in the natal chart are reflected in this solar return chart, sometimes with more favourable aspects. This suggests an integrative year with opportunities to use positively many of the indicators in the birth chart.

Transiting Sun passed over the solar return Midheaven in early January 1981, well before the actual announcement of the engagement, but perhaps important decisions were being made behind the scenes at this time. The Sun came to the Ascendant in late April, with no apparent earth-shattering revelation, but it was applying to a conjunction with the fourth house angle at the time of the

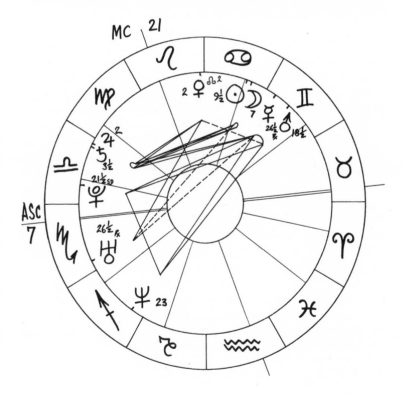

Figure 12. Princess Diana: Solar Return Chart, 1 July 1981.

wedding. In late October the Sun reached the seventh house angle and it may have been then that Prince Charles knew he was to become a father—the announcement that the Princess was expecting was made on 5 November 1981. We can note that transiting Moon had just passed the Descendant when the engagement was announced (24 February) and had just moved into the fourth house on the day of the wedding.

The Princess of Wales—Solar Return 1981/1982 and Lunar Return July/August 1981

Princess Diana's solar return for the year that included her marriage and will include the birth of her first child (at the time of writing the baby is due around her 1982 birthday) is shown on page 141 (Figure 12). It is not so dramatic an example as her husband's solar return and is therefore not so easy to interpret, but it is a useful exercise and we must remember that the chart reflects the year of which eleven months were after the wedding, and again it refers to Princess Diana herself in her new life and not necessarily how we see the public figure.

The birth chart shows some emphasis on the seventh and eighth houses and both the solar return rulers (Pluto and Mars) are in the natal eighth house; Mars is also in the solar return eighth house, conjunct Mercury, reflecting the natal sextile. Princess Diana is a person for whom marriage and close personal relationships are shown from her birth chart as being important, but in the year under examination emphasis moves to the eighth house—other people's feelings and possessions, sex, birth, money, the deeper, intimate, more complex aspects of relationship. The Moon is also technically in the eighth house and it is applying to the conjunction with the Sun, a new Moon, suggesting integration of masculine and feminine principles and a new beginning taking place during the year. The ninth house Sun and Venus (ruler of the seventh house) are puzzling and the placing could be interpreted in various ways. Travel is a possibility during the year or an increased involvement with religion and the church. The wedding itself was a splendidly ecumenical affair, but perhaps now as a member of the royal family she is having to become a more regular attender of Sunday worship than she may have been before. Perhaps the chart is pointing to deeper, more philosophical thought or even some form of private further education—there is a behind-the-scenes quality in the twelfth house placing of ruler Pluto. The ninth house is the house of long-term planning, in her case largely out of her hands, but it is also the house of parents-in-law and the Queen and Prince Philip are likely to be significant people in her life during her first year of marriage, perhaps acting as tutors in the skills of being a member of the royal family.

The solar return Ascendant is Scorpio and it falls in the tenth house in her natal chart, emphasizing her new position in society and, falling close to Neptune, it brings out glamour and perhaps an idealized attitude. It also reflects her husband's Scorpio Sun square Pluto and it is coincidently within orbs of a conjunction with Prince Charles' solar return seventh house angle and Mercury and it is exactly conjunct his natal Mercury—communication within the relationship should therefore be good. Personal change is indicated by Uranus in the first house, but it is without the difficult T-square emphasis seen in the birth chart, although the natal semi-square to the Sun is reflected by a sesquiquadrate. Natal Venus square Uranus is softened to a trine aspect in the solar return. The Jupiter/ Saturn conjunction moves into much more prominence and represents quite a frustrating factor in the return chart. It is in the eleventh house of more detached contacts with other people and could point to the opportunities and the restrictions which must occur with both old friends and new acquaintances. Where this conjunction refers natally to personal feelings and possessions, in the first year of marriage there is a much more extroverted emphasis concerning groups, affiliations, objectives and ideals—in short, many aspects of royal duties in public. The new horizons, coupled with the restrictions, are shown further as frustrations by the squares to Sun, Moon and Mercury.

The Leo Midheaven is appropriately regal, but there are no planets in the tenth house. The fact that one chart ruler, Pluto, is in the twelfth house suggests that there is much going on privately within the new Princess, an inner transformation which links with the deeper-thinking element of the ninth house emphasis in the chart. To suddenly undergo a major life change, becoming a member of the royal family and giving birth to an heir to the throne, could well give much to ponder on.

Looking at the timing indicators within the return chart itself we see the Sun transiting square the Ascendant at the time of the wedding, with Moon and Mars passing over the Sun/Moon conjunction at the same time. The solar transits of the angles only reveal a contact with the Ascendant just before the announcement of her pregnancy—the Moon moved over the fourth house angle on the day of the announcement. There were no other obvious events. For the record: Sun conjunct Midheaven—mid-August 1981; conjunct I.C.—mid-February 1982; conjunct Descendant—late April 1982. Princess Diana's solar return for the *previous* year—a year of great excitement and increasing activity for her—shows Jupiter exactly conjunct the Ascendant and Venus in the tenth house; the Sun was transiting the Descendant on the day of the announcement of her engagement. It will be seen that the Sun's transit over the solar return angles is a capricious indicator and it is statistically dubious. For instance, if one allows wide orbs of ±5°, more than 10 per cent of the year (40° out of 360°) is covered and it increases the probability of events that appear to correlate with the indicator. Movement of the Moon over the angles occurs thirteen times each year and is statistically even less reliable, so very tight orbs should be taken. Where forecasting or experimental work is carried out using this method, I recommend minimal orbs for the Moon and 2° for the Sun.

Princess Diana's lunar return covering the month of the wedding is included with some hesitation (see Figure 13). It seems fairer to stay with the example subjects rather than to scour the ephemeris for a lunar return which shows some amazing correlation in the life of a separate and specially selected person. I have not examined her other twelve lunar returns for 1981/82 and so I am unable to say whether a different month apparently announces marriage clearly and emphatically. Certainly there is little in this lunar return obviously suggesting it, but we must remember that the monthly return is subsidiary to the solar return—and Princess Diana's solar return did not announce marriage particularly strongly either; the chart suggested that the twelve months from July 1981 would emphasize relationship, change, new horizons and some frustrating restrictions.

Perhaps the most striking observation is that there is remarkable similarity between the lunar chart and the solar one. Admittedly the former's date is less than three weeks after the latter, so some planetary sign positions will be similar; but there is around a 60-1 chance that the two Ascendants would be within 3° of each other. Thus, the early part of Scorpio is a theme running through these three return charts applying to the wedding; Prince Charles' natal Mercury, his solar return Mercury and his solar return Descendant, Princess Diana's solar and lunar return Ascendants all

Figure 13.   Princess Diana: Lunar Return Chart, 19 July 1981.

come between 3½° and 7° Scorpio—and these degrees fall in her natal tenth house not far from her tenth house Neptune (8½°). Also, the simple coinciding of rising signs is a strong pointer to an important month.

The tenth house Venus in the lunar return chart, ruling the seventh house, takes on more meaning than is immediately obvious —love, harmony, and marriage with career, public image and position in the world. Venus is the only planet, apart from the Moon itself and Mercury, that has changed house from the solar return. Uranus remains in the first house suggesting personal change; the chart rulers Pluto and Mars remain in twelfth and eighth houses respectively, confirming the deeper elements of personal relationship, but with more private and secret emotions than outsiders might have imagined at the time. The Jupiter/Saturn conjunction, even closer by this time, continues to demand

and frustrate from its eleventh house position and the Sun sits enigmatically in the ninth house—church, royal in-laws, new horizons or merely travel on a famous private yacht. The solar return sesquiquadrate from Sun to Uranus eases to a trine, the Sun/ Moon conjunction becomes a quincunx and the squares to Saturn and Jupiter change to a single square to transforming Pluto, ruling the chart from a hidden kingdom in the twelfth house. Another cryptic indicator is the reappearance of the birth chart T-square involving Moon, Venus and Uranus, here with the opposition axis falling in the tenth and fourth houses.

Where other solar returns do present a relatively obvious statement for the year in question and can be interpreted in whatever degree of depth desired, lunar returns have a greater subtlety, which makes them more difficult to interpret. There are two charts to compare with (birth chart and solar return chart, with the latter being more relevant in this context), and the traditional concept of the lunar return as a timing indicator is not always obvious. Detailed interpretive examination has to be carried out in order to obtain timing clues.

Prince Charles—32nd Harmonic Chart

Prince Charles was engaged and married at the age of 32 and his 32nd harmonic chart is illustrated in Figure 14. The most outstanding feature of this chart is that the Sun, always a key factor, but here also Charles' natal Ascendant ruler, is closely angular in the part of the chart corresponding to the seventh house of partnerships and marriage, close to the degree of his natal Sun. At the same time it is almost exactly trine Uranus, ruler of his natal seventh house, which is conjunct the benefic Jupiter, ruler of the natal fifth house. This is a clear-cut indication of a year in which love and marriage will stir, motivate and awaken the psyche.

In addition, the Midheaven is with Mars, the male sex drive, in opposition to the Moon and square Venus, the two main feminine aspects of the psyche. It is a year in which there is shown the need to take action (Mars) in coming to terms with the feminine element in his life. Pluto conjunct the Ascendant, in a grand trine with Venus and Saturn, suggests a year of transformation and crystallized affections. We can also note that the harmonic Ascendant exactly conjuncts Princess Diana's Venus and the opposition to the Sun aspects her T-square. The Mars Midheaven opposite the Moon falls from Gemini to Sagittarius, correlating with Charles' various

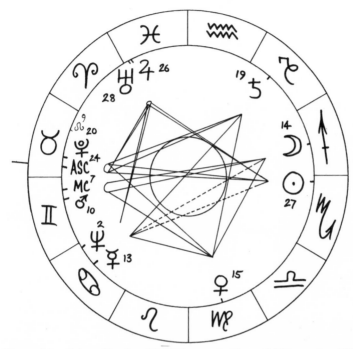

Figure 14. Prince Charles: 32nd Harmonic Chart, 14 November 1980.

riding accidents during the year and the loss of his favourite horse. The Mars/Moon/Venus T-square suggests the tension between assertive virility and a more receptive feminine harmonizing energy. It may also indicate the symbolic clash and break with the mother which marriage inevitably precipitates at some level, conscious or unconscious.

Saturn falls in Capricorn, the sign of duty, responsibility and serious achievement, and trines both the Ascendant and its ruler Venus—stability both personally and in relationship matters. Venus is emphasized in various ways, as might be expected; it is chart ruler and it is at the apex of both T-square and grand trine. It is also in the fourth house area from the Ascendant and in the first house area from the Midheaven, again pointing to relationship and family life. The Moon underlines the latter, being in the fourth house area from the Midheaven.

10.
FINAL WORDS

Astrology is not a precise science and forecasting by astrology is one of the less clear-cut aspects of the subject. Perfection, however, can belong only to the gods and we mere mortals must settle for something subordinate, so it is appropriate, in concluding this book, to turn to a myth which is less defined than most and concerns men as well as gods.

The sons and daughters of the Titans were many and Zeus, son of Kronos (Saturn), was the most powerful. One of his cousins was Prometheus, the one who foresees; Epimetheus was the brother, who reflects after the event. There are a number of different stories associated with Prometheus and many variations. He was a demigod who had a particular interest in the affairs of men, acting as a sort of intermediary with the gods. Later versions tell how he actually created the first man out of earth and water—some say with his own tears. He stole fire from the gods and gave it to men, for which Zeus sought revenge by creating the beautiful Pandora —her name means 'gift of all', but she was perfidious. He sent her to the world of men with a sealed vase, but Prometheus rejected her, being suspicious of any gift from angry Zeus. However, she enchanted Epimetheus who allowed her to stay with him. Later, her curiosity getting the better of her, she lifted the lid of the vase and released, in the shape of terrible demons, all the evils which were to henceforth plague and beset mankind. She quickly closed the lid, but only succeeded in retaining Hope which was saved as a comfort for man. Zeus finally satisfied his revenge by having Prometheus chained to a peak on Mount Caucasus, where an eagle daily ate out his liver—the organ being magically renewed each night. The demi-god was finally rescued by Hercules.

Fire was not Prometheus's only gift to men. He gave them the mechanical arts and, by giving medicines and healing drugs, took away the expectancy of death. He also endowed men with the divine gift of foresight. 'I drew clear lines for divination', Prometheus says in Aeschylus' play, 'and discerned what from dreams is sure to come to pass in waking. I disclosed the mysteries of omen-bringing words, and pathway tokens, and made plain the flight of taloned birds, both of good augury and adverse . . . I cleared the way for mortals to an art of hand discernment, and made bright fire-auguries, heretofore obscure and blind.' Although he apparently did not have anything to do with astrology, the gifts that he brought gave men the desire—and perhaps the means—to see the future.

In the sciences, foretelling the future has a respectability not enjoyed by astrology. If a scientist or economist is wrong in his predictions, he is just a person in error. The false prophet, however, is either a deceiving imposter or a misguided lunatic—and to many rationally-minded sceptics, astrologers are frequently seen as false prophets. The most common example of accepted future-gazing is the established science of meteorology. The statements on television and radio vary from categoric weather predictions in England to forecasts stating percentage probability in the USA. However much people may complain about the inaccuracies, the public generally believes in the system. This reveals the element of faith that is always present with any method of forecasting. Doctor, economist or weatherman, demi-gods of the twentieth century, all instill a certain degree of faith in those for whom they tell of future happenings.

The astrological forecaster, unless he is a charlatan, has faith in his methods, as will the person who consults him; but faith implies religious belief and there is always a danger that astrology may receive projections which turn it into a quasi-religion. Thus our future-gazing astrologer may be put into the role of high priest and be tempted to usurp the gods. Perhaps this is why, in mythology, the gods used to begrudge man too clear a vision of the future—it gave him too much power. Indeed, the basis of Zeus' anger towards Prometheus was that the fire-thief had some knowledge of Zeus' future and refused to divulge it.

All ancient oracles had a certain ambiguity about them, so that interpretation was probably more important than the utterance itself. Herodotus tells of the decisions that had to be made concerning the defence of Athens. The oracle was consulted and it gave the reply: 'Safe shall the wooden wall continue for thee and thy children'. Some people thought this meant that the citadel would be safe behind a palisade, but others maintained that it referred to the importance of the fleet—the latter was the interpretation which won acceptance and the decision led Athens towards becoming a maritime power. Thus information was presented in a way which gave the men opportunity for choice. If such choice did not exist, then mortal lives would be merely vehicles for the outward expression of the shifting balance of power on Mount Olympus; the gods would bind men together in comradeship or conflict and pull the ends of the rope back and forth at their whim. This model of existence or philosophy of life may have been appropriate for primitive man and, in today's world, it may appear attractive to timid and immature people unwilling to take on responsibility, but such a binding is indeed a restriction to real living.

Astrological forecasting reflects these choices. Either we can see the moving indicators in the birth chart as the ropes and chains that hold us back or drag us unavoidably in a direction decided by an outside agency; or, alternatively, we can take the progressions and transits as if they are the words of a sophisticated and highly specific oracle—not one which coquettishly refuses to give a coherent answer or interpretation, but one which presents a range of possibilities. It gives a set of tools, explains the many different ways they can be used and then hands them over to the individual so that he or she may use them creatively and industriously for a person-ally chosen purpose.

The astrologer's relationship with forecasting can be seen to loosely parallel the male child's growth to maturity, the symbolic hero's journey. When the child is born he needs the nurturing of the mother so that he can emerge from the undifferentiated chaos of his creation and begin to perceive separateness in life and his en-vironment. Soon he needs to become independent and to separate from the real mother and from the associated archetypal material and, modelling himself on the image of a positive father, assert his individuality so that he may go out into the world, perform his heroic deeds and eventually re-unite with the positive aspects of the parental archetypes. One attitude to astrological forecasting is still in the grip of the mother archetype. It is allowing oneself to be consumed by the devouring mother, sucked back into the womb where the astrologer (male or female) is impotent and castrated. The moving astrological indicators can supply every answer; no individual responsibility need be taken; only homage and sacrifice must be made to the ephemeris goddess before any action or decision is contemplated in life. Forecasting in the mould of the father archetype is perhaps a fixation on the power that may be wielded by the astrologer. He feels he has stolen fire from the gods and by withholding his prophecy from Zeus, like Prometheus, he retains some control over the most powerful member of the pantheon.

Prometheus' fate was to be chained to a rock for an indefinite period. Some accounts say this was for thirty years, while others give thirty thousand years; but one Saturn return or one thousand of them, it makes little difference unless the lessons are learned. Some astrologers are like this, stuck on a distant mountain peak, head in the clouds, presuming to defy the gods with omnipotent predictive declarations; but they are chained by their own hubris. Even under the torture of having his liver torn out daily by the eagle, Prometheus was unrepentant. The liver was the divinatory centre in haruspicy (entrail reading) and the vicious circle of the daily consumption of Prometheus' liver and its nightly regrowth reflects the inflexible, blinkered attitudes of our Promethean astrologer.

Prometheus was eventually rescued by Hercules, a hero who achieved a greater variety of adventures than most of his counterparts and who fulfilled many tasks. He made blunders and suffered humiliations, but he learned much—as we astrologers can learn through our own experiences, our astrological adventures and our sometimes imperfect handling of the moving planetary indicators. After his rescue Prometheus relented and told Zeus the information he had previously witheld—he was only a demi-god, but he would now, with Zeus' approval, be able to achieve divine immortality, if he could find another being to take on his mortality. The centaur Chiron agreed to do this to save himself from the pain and despair of an incurable wound. Thus it was this creature—half-man, half-horse, gentle healer, tutor to such a list of heroes it was like a roll of honour—who enabled Prometheus, trickster and foreteller, benefactor of mankind, to be elevated to the gods. Ironically, Hercules, the very saviour who killed the liver-eating eagle, had accidentally shot the poisoned arrow which incurably injured Chiron. Zeus eventually took Chiron from Hades and put him in the sky as the constellation Sagittarius.

The story twists and turns and doubles back on itself, not unlike the way in which we take our astrological forecasting indicators and try to shape coherent statements out of the multitude of possibilities. There are elements in the story of confronting the gods and being reconciled with them, of rebellion and trickery, of sacrifice and reward and of the hero's progress through trial and error and experience. In our own journeys towards increased consciousness and greater personal responsibility, we are wise to still recognize and respect the gods, but we need no longer be so much at their mercy. Astrological knowledge may be able to chain a person to the eagle's rock and it may even have some qualities of Pandora's sealed vase, but, with enlightened attitudes, knowledge and study of the moving planetary indicators can help people to contribute to the spinning of their own life threads and to stand with the Fates at the loom, having at least some say in the weaving of their own destinies and in the unfolding of the cloth of their lives on Earth.

BIBLIOGRAPHY

There are a vast number of books on astrology and many of them are on forecasting and prediction, so it is difficult to produce a manageable list. I have tried to give the better books on forecasting, but I also include a wide selection of subjects. Short comments are given on each.

Arroyo, S. *Astrology, Karma and Transformation* (C.R.C.S.). Profound and comprehensive, this book covers all aspects of forecasting—cycles, progressions and transits. Do not be misled or put off by the title.

Baigent, M., Campion, N., Harvey, C. *Mundane Astrology: An Introduction to the Astrology of Nations and Groups* (Aquarian Press, 1983). Includes information on the mundane aspects of cycles.

Carter, C. *Symbolic Directions* (originally published by Foulshams). Considers a range of directions based on various numerical quantities.

Davison, R. *The Technique of Prediction* (Fowler). A comprehensive range of interpretations is given—thorough and perceptive, but more event-oriented than psychological. Some of the techniques are complex and obscurely idiosyncratic.

Deluce, R. *The Complete Method of Prediction* (Deluce, 1962). Traditional approach, mainly covering primary directions.

De Vore, N. *Encyclopaedia of Astrology* (Littlefield Adams). Useful general compendium, which includes many aspects of forecasting and cycles.

Doane, D. *Progressions in Action* (A.F.A.). Short articles giving case histories of progressions operating for well-known people.

Dobyns, Z. *Progressions, Directions and Rectification* (T.I.A.). Useful, readable book covering straightforward rectification in some detail. Tertiary tables are included and pre-natal epoch is covered briefly.

Ebertin, R. *The Annual Diagram. Directions. Transits* (A.F.A.). These three books from the Ebertin mid-point school include use of the 45° ephemeris. Interpretations are based on research, but often seem pessimistic. Use with the handbook *Combination of Stellar Influences*.

Hand, R. *Planets in Transit* (Para Research). A very comprehensive work on transits covering all planetary contacts and movement through houses. The introduction contains useful general comments.

Harvey, C. *Harmonic Directions* (Sofia). Handbook on forecasting using harmonics. See also John Addey's original treatise *Harmonics in Astrology*.

Jayne, C. *Progressions and Directions* (priv. pub. Astrological Bureau). Covers a range of methods, some complex and obscure.

Jones, M. E. *The Scope of Astrological Prediction* (Sabian). Philosophical approach to forecasting, with examples, but somewhat convoluted.

Jinni and Joane. *When Your Sun Returns* (Search). Readable and more up-to-date booklet on solar returns.

Kemp, C. *Progressions* (Astrological Association). Booklet giving the method for calculating secondary and tertiary progressions, with tables, and a brief discussion of astronomical bases. Almost entirely technical in scope.

Leo, A. *The Progressed Horoscope* (Fowler). Old-fashioned, but a useful reference on primary directions. Not for the beginner.

Mann, T. *The Round Art. The Time of Your Life*. The first is a general book, but includes the author's own system of forecasting by logarithmic time scale. The second elaborates on this and links with the mid-point system.

Michelsen, N. *Astro Computing Services Catalog* (POB 16430, San Diego). Briefly describes a wide range of forecasting techniques. The calculation service extends from the simplest secondary progressions to harmonic charts and graphic transits or progressions to any scale (e.g. 45°) and in colour.

Robertson, M. *The Transits of Saturn* (Astrology Center, Seattle). Covers the transits and cycles of Saturn in great detail.

Rudhyar, D. *The Lunation Cycle* (Shambhala). Mainly natal considerations of the Moon and its phases, but cycles and lunar approaches to forecasting are also covered.

Ruperti, A. *Cycles of Becoming* (C.R.C.S.). Philosophical and practical book on the cycles of the planets, both individually and in pairs and other groupings.

Schwickert, G. *Rectification of the Birth Time* (A.F.A.). Of technical and academic interest on rectification in general. Covers the pre-natal epoch in detail.

Townley, J. *Astrological Cycles and Life Crisis Periods* (Weiser). Covers a range of cycles, building pictorially to a composite graph and relates them to life periods.

Tyl, N. *Integrated Transits. Analysis and Prediction* (Llewellyn). The first covers transits; the second is mainly essays on horary and electional astrology.

Volguine, A. *The Technique of Solar Returns* (A.S.I.). Somewhat old-fashioned book on solar returns.

Williamsen, J. *Harmonic Chart Tables* (A.F.A.). Tables for facilitating the calculation of harmonics.

INDEX

The Faculty of Astrological Studies

The Faculty of Astrological Studies was founded in 1948 for the purpose of improving astrological knowledge and raising standards through courses of tuition and by examinations. There are correspondence courses for both Certificate and Diploma levels, offering personal tuition of a high standard to students anywhere in the world and evening classes are also held in London, England. Certificate and Diploma exams take place each year and are open to Faculty students and others alike. The Diploma of the Faculty (D.F.Astrol.S.) is internationally recognized and is one of the most respected astrological qualifications in the world.

For further details write to:

The Registrar,
Faculty of Astrological Studies,
Hook Cottage,
Vines Cross,
Heathfield,
Sussex.